W9-DGI-024

Questioning
Skills for the Helping Process

Questioning
Skills for the Helping Process

Lynette Long
Loyola College in Maryland

Louis V. Paradise
The Catholic University of America

Thomas J. Long
The Catholic University of America

Brooks/Cole Publishing Company
Monterey, California

Library
S.W. Ok. St. U
Weatherford, Oklahoma

Brooks/Cole Publishing Company
A Division of Wadsworth, Inc.

© 1981 by Wadsworth, Inc., Belmont, California 94002.
All rights reserved. No part of this book may be reproduced,
stored in a retrieval system, or transcribed, in any form or by any means—
electronic, mechanical, photocopying, recording, or otherwise—
without the prior written permission of the publisher,
Brooks/Cole Publishing Company, Monterey, California 93940,
a division of Wadsworth, Inc.

Printed in the United States of America

10 9 8 7 6 5 4 3 2 1

Library of Congress Cataloging in Publication Data

Long, Lynette.
    Questioning : skills for the helping process.

    Includes bibliographical references and index.
    1. Questioning.   2. Helping behavior.
3. Counseling   I. Paradise, Louis V., 1946-
joint author.   II. Long, Thomas J., 1938-   joint
author.   III. Title.
BF637.H4L66   158'.3   80-24385
ISBN 0-8185-0371-8

Acquisition Editor: *Claire Verduin*
Manuscript Editor: *Julie Segedy*
Production Editors: *Marilu Uland and Patricia E. Cain*
Interior and Cover Design: *Katherine Minerva*
Cover Photograph: *Stan Rice*
Typesetting: *Instant Type, Monterey, California*

158.3
L852q

To our parents:
John and Margaret
Louis and Lucille
Albert and Anita
who are still asking appropriate questions

247324

Preface

This book is designed to give individuals in the helping professions a basic understanding of the skills of appropriate questioning, because questions can greatly facilitate the various stages and goals of the counseling process.

Although most instructional materials on counseling techniques advise the student counselor to limit or avoid the use of questions, considerable evidence indicates that questioning is frequently an effective verbal-interaction technique. Indeed, questions may be considered a primary tool in most counseling and therapy situations.

The text makes a comprehensive examination of the uses and misuses of questions. Using a developmental model for counseling, the text provides the reader with specific strategies as they related to (a) client exploration, (b) problem identification and integration, and (c) client action.

The text can readily be used as a supplementary text for helping professionals in a variety of disciplines such as counseling, nursing, psychiatry, psychology, and social work. The text discusses the role of questions in counseling and ways to discriminate between appropriate and inappropriate questions. We demonstrate the use of questions in the counseling process and provide numerous examples of useful strategies. A component on self-evaluation is also included at the end of each skill-building chapter. Many examples of actual practice are included throughout the text, as well as two chapters on special uses for questions in the structured interview and with the nonverbal client. The final chapter provides group simulation exercises on the appropriate use of questions.

There are several people who have been of assistance to us in the preparation of this text. Our thanks go to the reviewers: Meryl Englander, of Indiana University; Bruce Fretz, of the University of Maryland; Allen E. Ivey, of the University of Massachusetts; Paul Kessler, of Delaware Technical and Community College; Beverly B. Palmer, of California State University at Dominguez Hills; Fred Pearman, of South Oklahoma City Junior College; Peter Racheotes, of East Texas State University at Texarkana; and Carl D. Swanson, of James Madison University.

We are also grateful to Claire Verduin, Marilu Uland, and Katherine Minerva, of the editorial staff at Brooks/Cole, for providing valuable counsel and advice and for their patience. Finally, we would like to express our appreciation to Barbara Howard, who deciphered countless pages of pen-scratchings and turned them into a typed manuscript.

Lynette Long
Louis V. Paradise
Thomas J. Long

Contents

Questioning
Skills for the Helping Process

1

Questions: A Neglected Counseling Tool

QUESTIONS: FACILITATIVE OR INHIBITING?

Why is there a need for a book on the use of questions in counseling? No one else has considered it necessary to devote an entire book to this topic. In fact, questions generally have been dismissed as "unacceptable" messages that block effective interpersonal communication (Gordon, 1974).

In most counseling training programs that teach a counseling process based on interpersonal dialogue and development of the client/counselor relationship, questioning is the part of the counseling process that is ignored. Those who teach counseling generally consider questioning a mark of a low-functioning practitioner and, rather than developing it as a useful art, criticize students for asking questions during counseling sessions.

Those authors who do address the use of questions markedly limit the positive application of questioning in the counseling dialogue, while spending considerable time spelling out the deleterious effects questions can have on the client/counselor relationship (Gazda, Asbury, Balzer, Childers, & Walters, 1977). Nowhere outside the literature on constructing surveys and conducting content interviews is questioning developed as a positive tool. Yet questioning is one of the most basic and prevalent forms of interpersonal response. It is a natural form of communication—a universal skill that all individuals learn but, as an art, few master.

Human beings rely heavily on questions in their social interactions. Questions are used to communicate interest, to express lack of understanding, and to share a concern. They are also used to threaten, to confront, and to demonstrate superiority. The uses of questions are as diverse as the consequences of questioning, and questions can facilitate communication or inhibit it.

1

It is, perhaps, precisely because questioning can work for good or ill in the counseling relationship that it has been so neglected as a useful counseling skill. In trying to limit the counterproductive aspects of questioning, many counseling approaches have virtually tried to eliminate it.

Gerard Egan (1975) links questioning with a low level of functioning: "Low-level counselors ask too many questions and try to substitute questions for accurate empathy in their efforts to get the client to explore himself" (p. 88). Results reported by Carkhuff (1969a) imply somewhat the same thing: "Experienced, low-functioning practitioners [tended] to be either directive or to ask questions (often irrelevant if not stupid questions)" (p. 103). Gordon (1974) strongly indicts questioning as unacceptable; of the 12 categories of messages he lists that block further communication, he says that the most frequently used is questioning. Even Benjamin (1969), who has given questioning the most extensive consideration in the counseling literature, is full of reservations about its use:

> Yes, I have many reservations about the use of questions in the [helping] interview. I feel certain that we ask too many questions, many meaningless ones. We ask questions that confuse the interviewee, that interrupt him. We ask questions the interviewee cannot possibly answer. We even ask questions we don't want the answers to, and, consequently, we do not hear the answers when forthcoming [pp. 62–63].

Yet all of these authors acknowledge that questioning is part of human relations and, as such, cannot be separated from counseling. Counselors will continue to ask questions of clients, and clients will ask questions of counselors. It seems more in keeping with professional growth to systematically teach the appropriate use of questioning than to artificially constrain the use of one of the most prevalent forms of interpersonal response. The professional who knows how to use questioning as a tool will not need to eliminate it from his or her repertoire or be constantly cautioned against its misuse.

Indeed, the use of questions in counseling is currently experiencing a kind of a rebirth. Long (1975), in comparing various response styles of interviewers, found not only that questioning was the most frequent mode of communication but that interviewees felt most understood by interviewers whose predominant response style was questioning. In applying to counseling the work of Anderson (Anderson & Biddle, 1975) regarding adjunct questioning, Marshall (1976) found that clients can be helped to remember what went on in their individual counseling sessions long after the session's end through the counselor's use of adjunct questions. These results were in marked contrast to those obtained with clients who did not experience adjunct questioning.

Questioning is a major cognitive tool in counseling. It can help both the counselor and the client to sort out the hundreds of events, both verbal and nonverbal, that occur every few seconds in interpersonal communication. Questions, appropriately used, can help the counselor and client to understand which events provide pertinent information that should be focused on and remembered and which should be bypassed.

The Long (1975) study even casts doubt on the general belief that questioning interferes with the counseling atmosphere in which a warm, trusting relationship develops. It is true that a climate of acceptance is necessary for a positive counseling outcome, but it is not necessary to eliminate all confrontation and querying in order to achieve this climate. The appropriate use of questions can enhance trust and develop in the client a feeling of having been understood and cared for. A facilitative relationship may even *depend* on the selective use of questions.

It is our intent to demonstrate that the appropriate use of questions can have beneficial consequences for counseling. We believe that effective questioning is a critical interpersonal skill for counselors to master. While we do not suggest that questioning should be the dominant response employed in the counseling dialogue—indeed, we do not believe that any response should be used exclusively—we do suggest that there are times in any counseling interaction when questioning will be the preferred response. Counselors who consistently avoid the use of questions limit a natural human response and will eventually appear stilted to the client.

This book will identify and demonstrate the conditions under which questions can facilitate counseling and the conditions under which they can inhibit it. We have set forth training procedures to assist counselors in acquiring proficiency in formulating questions and in identifying their appropriate use. We also have provided simulations through which instructors may assess and enhance the questioning skills of their students.

QUESTIONING: A COMPLEX SKILL

The effective use of questioning is a complex skill to master. Its complexity arises from the fact that it (a) may both assist and inhibit the counseling relationship, (b) may establish either a desired or an undesired pattern of interpersonal exchange, and (c) may place the client in the position either of being interrogated or of being understood by the counselor. Questioning may also create a situation in which the counselor, now equipped with the client's answers, is expected to provide a solution to the client's problem or risk being rejected as incompetent.

The confusion about effective questioning arises long before formal counseling training begins. Emotional responses to questioning and the use of questioning as more than a tool for collecting information are experienced early in life, and they are not easily unlearned in adulthood. Questioning begins in childhood as part of the process of discovering the world and arriving at a better understanding of the self in relation to it. Children ask question after question in their efforts to get information, investigate causes, and understand reasons. Questions used in this manner are appropriate. Indeed, there is no substitute for them. Adults, although occasionally annoyed by the barrage of questions from their children, are generally pleased by their search for understanding and feel positive about this kind of questioning. Such questioning can elevate the self-esteem of both participants as the child acquires new and interesting information and the adult earns the child's admiration and respect as the source of the information.

It is only later that we learn that questions can carry moral judgments. Children learn from adults that questions can be used to put them on the spot, to get them to indict themselves for disapproved behavior, or to confuse them with complex choices. Questions thus become confusing.

Once we have learned the varied uses of questioning, we begin to evaluate questions against an emotional backdrop. Naturally enough, we react to questions in the way we have learned to react to them over the years: we defend ourselves against them, and we use them to produce a variety of results.

To develop questioning skills that bring positive results in counseling, the existing, habitual response patterns frequently have to be extinguished and new responses learned. Even something as basic as being aware that a question is being asked has to be increased. The counselor must also learn to assess the desirability of asking a question in a given situation or under specific circumstances. The counselor must know the various kinds of questions that can be used and the kinds that he or she most often uses.

In addition, counselors must learn to make their feelings and their meanings clearer to clients when they use questions, especially at the outset of the counseling relationship. This greater clarity will help the client learn to respond to the question being asked, rather than responding in habitual ways to the fact of being questioned. As the client and counselor develop their relationship and as questioning plays an increasingly significant part in that relationship, the fears about negative effects of questioning will gradually diminish.

The challenge of this book is (a) to help the reader develop an understanding of the many kinds of questions available and the impact of each kind, (b) to demonstrate how to formulate questions and when to use them, and (c) to help the reader acquire the skills of effective questioning in counseling. By mastering the art of questioning, you will add a powerful tool to your professional repertoire.

This text contains several types of instructional materials. The theory of questioning and its relationship to the counseling process is presented in a standard, didactic format. Each of the phases of exploration, integration, and action are presented in depth, with illustrations of the appropriate questioning style. Programmed exercises are provided to demonstrate the various types of questions in action, and the implications of each type of question are considered. Much of the theory and many of the concepts in the text are presented in the context of these exercises; therefore, maximum understanding of the material will be obtained only by reading and working all of the exercises. The text and exercises are cumulative and sequential: basic skills are presented and developed in the order in which they generally will be used during the counseling process.

The programmed materials are of two basic formats. Most of the items are branched, and these items include a client statement and three possible counselor responses from which to select the most appropriate. The response selected determines which page the reader next turns to. Each reader, therefore, reads a slightly different portion of the text. Many readers find it helpful after completing a section of the manual to go back and read all of the pages they were instructed to skip, thus getting a better understanding of why certain options were incorrect. The rest of the programmed items are linear. These items present a question, and the reader is to supply the correct answer. The answers to the questions are listed and explained on the page following the question. Readers will gain the greatest understanding of the concepts and of their own styles of questioning if they actually fill in the blanks and analyze their own questioning styles.

The text also contains two lengthy client/counselor dialogues. These are annotated, and they provide illustrations of the flow of questioning and its effect on the entire counseling process. The reader will benefit from studying these examples and from referring to them when reading the rest of the text.

Finally, the reader must practice the concepts presented in order to get maximum benefit from the text. Watching the reactions of the client as questions are asked can provide new insights into the effects of questioning in counseling. Only by integrating these new questioning skills into your existing counseling responses will these skills prove helpful.

The Role of Questions in Counseling

Questions constitute a large part of human interaction. Despite the risks inherent in their use, they can facilitate counseling interactions by inviting the client to speak, saving time, focusing the attention of the client, making general concepts more specific, or combining specific examples into general themes. Questions can help the client to process information on higher conceptual levels. They also can assist the counselor in sorting out the hundreds of events that occur in any one counseling session. Questions can even facilitate a warm, trusting climate in which two partners work together to arrive at mutually agreed upon goals.

THE CONTEXT OF COUNSELING

We will be discussing questioning in the context of counseling, which we define as a process of shared human interaction undertaken to resolve specific and agreed upon problems. Counseling is based on the establishment and maintenance of a facilitative relationship and demands the exchange of information, which leads to new learning, unlearning, or relearning for the client. The learning process then culminates and becomes observable as constructive changes in the client's behavior.

THE COUNSELING PROCESS

Formal counseling progresses through regular and interdependent phases, the success of each succeeding phase depending on the successful completion of the preceding phases. The process is outlined in incremental steps, although the phases of the process are not sharply delineated.

We will outline the phases of the counseling process in order to help you understand the process itself. Remember, however, that these phases of counseling are not independent of one another; they are overlapping, interdependent steps in the counseling process. As the counseling progresses, these steps are melded together into a unified whole.

Some people may believe that it's unrealistic to describe counseling as such a step-by-step process; that counseling is better carried out in a relatively illogical, emotionally loaded fashion; that any attempt to direct the client into progressing through counseling according to a predetermined order of events curtails the client's ability to think or talk about relevant issues (Patterson, 1974). We disagree with this criticism, believing that it is better to conduct counseling according to logical patterns. Our experience leads us to believe that clients are more likely to remember all aspects of an issue and cover it more thoroughly when the issue is approached systematically. Furthermore, clients are more likely to adapt favorably to their role and responsibilities in the counseling relationship if some indication is given them of what is expected of them during the counseling process (Hoehn-Saric, Frank, Imber, Nash, Stone, & Battle, 1964; T. J. Long, 1968; Truax & Carkhuff, 1967). The counselor should provide structure only to the extent necessary, however. If the client naturally adopts a reasonably sequential approach, there is no need for the counselor to do more than point out the sequence being followed.

PHASE 1: EXPLORATION

During the exploratory phase of the counseling process, the client and counselor exchange information about themselves. This information helps them to establish their relationship by defining their needs, goals, and responsibilities in the counseling effort. During this phase, questions are appropriate and are frequently used to invite client involvement in the process, to assist in establishing a genuine and comprehensible relationship, and to identify perceived areas of difficulty.

Phase 1 is composed of three interdependent levels of action: preparation and joining, establishment of a facilitative environment, and identification of the client's inappropriate life behavior and of the client's perceived problems. These levels are not likely to exist independent of one another, but we can examine them separately.

Level 1: Preparation and Joining

This level really begins before client and counselor first face each other. The counselor must already have developed an effective communication style and be acquainted with a workable theory of personality. He or she will use this theory to make sense of the multiple interactions that occur between counselor and client and, particularly, to understand which of the many events that occur are providing pertinent information. Also, the counselor must have a workable framework or model for counseling practice to help him or her translate the chosen theory of human personality into a practical strategy for helping.

The client must attain one or more of the following states during Level 1: a state of personal anxiety, a state in which the client's behavior becomes a significant annoyance to others, or a state in which the client has a heightened desire for increased personal growth. During this level, the client—by cautiously exploring the counseling environment—must answer the following questions in the affirmative:

1. Do I experience this counselor as able to understand me?
2. Do I trust that this person can be of help to me?
3. Do I choose to work with this counselor?

The counselor, by attending both to his or her own cues and to those of the client, must respond affirmatively to the following:

1. Do I feel capable of understanding what this person is trying to communicate to me?
2. Do I feel comfortable with the level of respect we have for each other?
3. Do I believe that I can be of help to this person?

It is only at the point at which each party is able to respond positively to these questions that real joining in the process of counseling is accomplished.

Level 2: Establishment of a Facilitative Environment

This level begins at the very moment when the client presents him or herself for help and it continues throughout the counseling. The establishment of a facilitative environment depends largely on the counselor's ability to communicate three necessary conditions: empathic understanding of the client, respect for the client, and genuineness. These conditions have been written about by Rogers (1951, 1957, 1961) and elaborated upon by Patterson (1973b). Considerable systematic research on these variables has substantiated their role as necessary conditions for constructive client change (Carkhuff & Berenson, 1977; Middlebrooks, 1975; Truax & Carkhuff, 1967; Truax & Mitchell, 1971).

Not only must these conditions be offered by the counselor, but also the extent to which they are offered must be perceived by the client. Rogers (1961) emphasized that significant learning in counseling cannot occur unless the *client* perceives that these conditions exist. It is not sufficient that they are apparent to an outside observer; they must be communicated to and acknowledged by the client.

The counselor can experience the feelings of empathy, respect, and genuineness without knowing whether the client is perceiving these feelings. The communication of the counselor's empathy, respect, and genuineness depends on (1) the skillful sequencing of verbal and nonverbal cues uniquely designed to suit the client and (2) the client's ability to receive the counselor's message. The counselor must find a way to assess how his or her feelings are being perceived by the client. Questions are usually the most direct and efficient way to make this assessment. The counselor may legitimately ask, "Do you feel that I am understanding what you want me to understand?" or "Are you comfortable with the way I show my respect for you?" or "Do you experience me as being honest when I communicate my feelings to you?"

Level 3: Identification of Appropriate and Inappropriate Client Behavior and the Client's Perceived Problems

The primary goal of the counseling at this level is that of client disclosure. The client reveals past and present behavior, needs, wants, concerns, and feelings. These behaviors, feelings, and experiences can be intuited by the counselor only to a very limited extent. It is only through client disclosure that they can be fully known to the counselor and adequately dealt with in the counseling sessions.

The counselor, however, is not entirely "at the mercy" of the client during Level 3. The counselor knows the key subjective and objective factors that influence how people relate to one another and has learned to use his or her own thoughts and feelings to further the communication process. The counselor should have a broad knowledge of the possible meanings of both verbal and nonverbal cues and be attentive to both types. If, in addition, the counselor has developed an understanding of logical processes and of the difficulties that clients encounter in disclosure, he or she might be able to judge whether the client is communicating with continuity or fully or honestly.

Questioning plays an important part in Level 3. Questions not only serve to stimulate disclosure but also to help the client elaborate a point, give examples, and narrate feelings. Questions are often the most expeditious and precise way to identify client behavior, experiences, and perceived areas of difficulty. To show interest, encourage the client to continue, or determine the completeness of a statement, a facilitative counselor might combine a statement and a question: "I heard you say your father left home very angry. What did you experience at that moment?" The question might bring out useful information as well as encourage the client to continue. The client might even gain insight from his or her own response: "I was angry too!"

This exploratory phase is essential; counseling cannot progress unless a certain amount of information is shared. Unfortunately, many counselors never go beyond this phase. They often cooperate with clients who want their problems catered to rather than resolved. By endlessly wandering in the exploratory phase, both counselor and client pretend that counseling is progressing—while a status quo palatable to the client is maintained. Many authors have pointed out that the frequent and undisciplined use of exploratory questions is the mark of an inept counselor.

An inept counselor might also be identified by the robot-like use of reflective responses. A skilled counselor will be as able to facilitate the counseling process through a well-placed question as through a reflective response. Counseling skill lies not in avoiding asking questions, but in their selection and timing.

PHASE 2: INTEGRATION

During the integration phase of counseling, the client moves toward an understanding of his or her own self, own world, and its difficulties—including the restraining and facilitating forces in his or her life. During this phase the client prepares for constructive behavior change. Questions are often used effectively during this phase to help the client express underlying assumptions, give specific examples, and outline goals and personal resources. The counselor also uses questions to help understand the themes and patterns of the client's behavior, verify inferences about the client, and become acquainted with the client's attitudes, emotions, motivations, and concept of self. Questions can elicit responses that resolve discrepancies perceived by the counselor and can help determine whether the client is ready to accept the possibility of effecting positive change in his or her behavior. Phase 2 is composed of three levels of action: analysis, encounter, and immediacy.

We have indicated that our concept of counseling is shared problem solving. During Phase 1 much of the sharing is from the client. The counselor tries to get enough of the pieces of the puzzle out on the table to be able to see themes and patterns of behavior. We try to help the client express not only problem areas, but underlying assumptions that may contribute to problems. We try to understand the client's goals and the values that determine how the client spends time and energy. We also attempt to determine the client's degree of anxiety, ability to control anxiety, and frequency of anxiety attacks.

During Phase 2 sharing is more balanced. While during Phase 1 the counselor frequently simply reflects what the client has said, in Phase 2 the counselor becomes more active and points out what the client has implied but not stated. The counselor not only obtains information, but also analyzes it and makes inferences about the client's behavior during counseling.

Output takes two forms during Phase 2. One form is tentative conclusions by the counselor at the end of the analysis: (a) identifying problem areas, (b) diagnosing the causes of the client's problems, (c) predicting how the client will behave in future situations, and (d) saying what might be done to help the client to organize and integrate his or her understanding of self, world, and the restraining and facilitating forces in his or her life, and to arrive at agreed on specific problem areas.

During this phase the qualities needed for establishing a facilitative environment are not neglected. The counselor combines empathic understanding and analytic skill to bring apparently isolated facts into clear focus for himself or herself and for the client. The counselor's genuineness is made evident by willingness to share experiences. And the counselor demonstrates respect by exploring his or her own immediate relationship with the client.

Level 1: Analysis

Communication in which one person requests information and another supplies it is common to all human experience. If a counselor is to help a client, he or she must know certain things about the client— the nature and duration of the complaints, the circumstances of the problem onset, whether emotional factors are involved, and so forth. But discrete bits of information must also be integrated and analyzed in order to get a complete picture of the client. The counselor's job at this level is to see the client's world as completely and with as much penetration as possible and then to relate this data back to the client in a useful way so that shared action can ensue.

Mr. Lowell: I heard you say that you love your mother very much and are very ill at ease with your father; and yet, when you had a chance to choose which parent you wanted to live with you chose your father. Am I missing some important piece of information that might help me understand this apparent inconsistency?

Alicia: I love my mother but she would have a hard time supporting me.

Mr. Lowell: Does that mean that your father is not obligated to pay something for your support?

Alicia: Oh, he is and does, but if I'm with my mother it's only so much, oh . . . $200 a month, I think.

Mr. Lowell: Can you help me understand why you made the choice you did?

Alicia: Well, oh, I know my mother doesn't make much and $200 just doesn't go very far. I mean, it barely covers my school expenses. Besides I'm not home all that much, and Dad is always a soft touch.

Mr. Lowell: Let's see . . . you judged that you would have more money available to you if you lived with your dad and perhaps experience less interference from either of your parents.

Alicia: That's about it!

Mr. Lowell: Would it be fair for me to infer that neither your desire to be with your mother nor your discomfort at being with your father is intense?

Alicia: Well, I'm pretty uncomfortable when I'm with my dad.

Mr. Lowell: When did you first begin noticing this discomfort?

Alicia: Well, my dad and I have never been real close but I guess I first began to feel uncomfortable after they separated. It got worse after I decided to live with him.

Mr. Lowell: Is it possible that you feel guilty or ashamed that you don't experience as much care for your father, from whom you are obviously accepting so much, as you do for your mother?

At this level of analysis, the counselor will frequently summarize the events to help the client understand him- or herself in an integrated and directed way. Summaries can identify the range of problems troubling the client, the resources he or she sees as available and the forces blocking problem resolution. They also make certain that the counselor understands the picture of the world held by the client.

The counselor can also use questions to bring into focus a confused and rambling narrative. The counselor attempts during this part of the counseling process to clear up inaccuracies and to clearly identify behavoral and emotional themes presented by the client. The counselor must make certain that he or she has correct data on which to proceed. If the counselor is accurate in his or her assumptions, it will have tremendous impact on changing the client's interpretations about certain people, objects, or events.

Level 2: Encounter or Confrontation

This level of counseling depends on the therapist's prior experience with the client. As usual, Level 2 activities are integrated with and related to counseling activities from other levels. Yet the type of activity outlined here needs additional preparation if it is to be effective, as premature encountering or confronting tend to be more risky.

At this level of encountering, the counselor can make the client aware of discrepancies that the counselor has heard between different client communications—verbal or nonverbal—or between the client's view of him- or herself and other's perceptions of the same situation. The counselor can also identify areas in which his or her perceptions of the world differ from the client's or of areas in which the client seems to be engaging in some destructive pattern of behavior.

During our lifetime we learn a variety of defense mechanisms, and these habitual, often primitive, reactions are easily elicited by confrontation or perceived threat. We therefore suggest that confrontation be approached cautiously, often in successive steps in order to keep from calling up the client's defense strategies. Confrontation can be a very useful tool in helping the client understand and integrate disowned parts of his or her being, but it will prove destructive if it causes the client to be defensive or resistant.

Gentle, successive questioning can help lead the client through learning steps to arrive at understanding. Such questioning can move from the concrete to the abstract, from the specific to the general. However, open-ended questions at this stage can be harmful if they intensify the client's projections of disaster or heighten his or her defenses instead of keeping them at a level more conducive to understanding and integration. We will discuss this point further later on, but for now, consider the following example:

Ms. Berg: You said that you would like to feel more in control of your job, yet you seem never to offer suggestions to your boss, co-workers, even subordinates.

The counselor could follow this statement with either of the following open questions, but only one of them actually maintains a positive atmosphere.

Mrs. Dow: Can you tell me more about this? [or] How do you feel hearing me say this?

This kind of open question is more likely to heighten a client's defenses and necessitate more established trust than the following parallel but more specific question:

Mr. Goldman: Can you recall times when you attempted to give suggestions? [or] What feelings seem to arise in you when you find yourself wanting to offer a suggestion?

Encountering is an important part of counseling. Avoiding confrontation limits the counselor's range of potential influence.

Level 3: Immediacy

This level has two purposes: (a) to help the client understand him- or herself through the continued relationship between client and counselor and (b) to help the client understand how behavior in counseling sessions indicates behavior outside counseling and suggest a starting point for change. Hopefully, the client will see the need for action on his or her part in the world outside of counseling.

Counselors must be aware of their own behavior if they are to help the client understand him- or herself better through their relationship. They must be able to openly and directly talk about their own actions and reactions and present their genuine responses to the client's problems. Oftentimes the client has arrived at a confused and painful state because the world did not seem to offer clear, open, and immediate communication. By processing the immediate counseling relationship, the client can become aware of growth-producing behavior. It is by relating present behavior to past and future behavior that the client can see continuity and the possibility of real and appropriate change.

While there is some chance that the client will attempt to block his or her own positive growth by defensively querying the counselor, we nonetheless encourage the client to ask questions. It is left to the counselor to know when client questions are facilitative or inhibiting. As clients learn that questions can be useful to their therapy, they will ask questions to make it seem less mysterious and more productive.

PHASE 3: ACTION

During this phase, established goals are met through the client's behavior change. Identifiable goals are first outlined, alternatives are listed and evaluated, and a plan of action is selected, implemented, and evaluated before the client attempts the next alternative solution. Phase 3 is composed of several interdependent levels that include:

1. Selecting a goal or prioritizing goals
2. Outlining alternatives for achieving each goal
3. Evaluating each alternative in light of the client's knowledge of self and of the constraining and facilitating forces perceived as being in the world
4. Selecting a plan of action from possible alternatives consistent with the client's value system
5. Implementing the plan of action selected
6. Evaluating the outcome of the client's new behavior in light of established criteria for success

7. Moving on to the next problem, reformulating the present problem, or implementing the next alternative by repeating steps 5 through 7 or 2 through 7 as required.

Level 1: Selecting and Prioritizing Goals

Clients often tend to identify their problems as someone else's and establish a goal of changing the behavior of a husband, wife, or employer. Counselors must remember that they cannot effect change in the behavior of people with whom they have no contact. The goal in counseling is problem resolution, but the resolution must involve constructive behavior change for the *client*, even if that means learning to live as effectively as possible in the face of adversity. A goal for behavior change should be formulated. Subgoals, if any, should be prioritized. If there is no prioritizing of subgoals, the sequence of responding could begin with (a) the most pressing problem, (b) the least severe problem, or (c) the problem that, if treated, will facilitate the maximum amount of improvement.

Level 2: Outlining Alternatives

At this point the counselor would encourage the client to explore as many alternatives as the client could think of, without criticizing any of them or judging their workability. This is what is meant by *brainstorming*, and it is a creative process, not an evaluative one. Evaluation of each possibility comes later. Counselors can help their clients understand that there are several possible solutions to most problems. It is important to remember that the solutions considered for implementation, however, must not be in conflict with the client's value system, because this would almost certainly make the solution fail.

Level 3: Evaluating Alternatives

Each alternative proposed should be evaluated for workability, based on the knowledge, resources, and possible obstacles of the client. Alternatives should also be evaluated in terms of the preconditions necessary in order to reach the desired outcome.

Level 4: Selecting a Plan of Action

Select the plan of action the client will follow first. Here the counselor is interested in the degree of commitment the client has to this plan.

Level 5: Implementing the Plan Selected

Implementation is left up to the client. Counselors should avoid the tendency to guarantee the success of any plan, and should not personally interfere with the client's execution of the plan.

Level 6: Evaluating the Outcome

Evaluate the outcome of the plan by first establishing criteria for success. This means encouraging the client to consider how he or she can recognize that progress has been made. This should be done before attempting to implement the action plan selected. Be certain that the action plan is stated so concretely that it can be measured in a tangible way.

Level 7: Moving On

Move on, reformulate, or attempt the next alternative solution. While we would hope that the therapy is so logically and carefully formulated that the first attempted solution succeeds, it does not always work that way. If the client has developed a sense of trust in the counselor and in the process, however, an initial failure will not harm the relationship.

In our concept of counseling, insight is not always enough. There must be changes in client behavior for counseling to be successful. While intrapersonal exploration is an important part of counseling, actual changes in client behavior must accompany or follow development of self-awareness. Self-exploration leads to self-awareness as well as to the client's understanding of his or her impact on other people and things. This understanding in turn becomes the basis on which the client begins to act in more facilitative ways. In other words, the client begins to act so that his or her behavior and self-understanding are congruent. This is frequently manifested first in the therapeutic setting itself as the client experiments with new behaviors with the counselor.

Self-exploration also reveals inconsistencies and contradictions in the client. The counselor uses questions to confront the client with attitudes, feelings, and behaviors that have been experienced but denied or distorted in awareness. As these aspects of the self become consciously symbolized, the client becomes more self-aware. Vague dissatisfactions become more specific. Furthermore, as the client becomes aware of specific dissatisfactions as well as specific abilities, plans of action can emerge that will allow the client to bring about more desirable behavior. Stated differently, as the client develops a stronger self-understanding in a safe environment, it will become increasingly important for him or her to bring behavior, attitudes, feelings, beliefs, and values into line in order to maintain internal congruence. The congruence provided by the counselor as a condition of therapy must become an integral part of the client's change. The counselor's questions can help the client through self-exploration. This will lead to other questions that help the client become aware of denied or distorted aspects of him- or herself and ultimately to questions that help the client bring his or her behavior into line with a more desired and accepted self.

Asking questions encourages the client to cognitively process his behavior, attitudes, feelings, beliefs, and values. A major critical client change follows from this cognitive understanding of self (Lieberman, Yalom, & Miles, 1973) and action on the part of the client (Carkhuff, 1969b). Understanding and action are interacting processes that often occur simultaneously (Carkhuff, 1969b). Either may precede or follow the other, depending on internal perceptions or external conditions. Specific behavior changes can occur as by-products of altered self-understanding and self-acceptance; changes in one's understanding and acceptance of self can also occur as a by-product of behavior change.

QUESTIONS

Questions are an important part of the shaping process of counseling. If used consciously, they become a powerful and useful part of the mutual process of counseling. Whether the client or the counselor leads together they progress toward increasingly understood and agreed-upon goals.

Questions help to model full human functioning. The counselor who only replies to questions, who avoids counseling leads, who labors through inconsistencies while the client tries to resolve his or her own questions, models an example of limited human relating. In successful counseling, the therapist models behaviors he or she hopes the client will exhibit. Such behaviors include asking questions as well as listening to them, disclosing information as well as understanding it, and resolving issues as well as tolerating them. In this context, questioning is not only a useful tool, but also an essential element to successful therapeutic interaction.

CAUTIONS

This book is about the use of questions in counseling, but we would like to briefly outline some cautions in their use. It is important to recognize that there are differences in types of questions. They do not fall into two distinct categories of open and closed. Instead, they run the gamut from situations in which there are a limited number of known frames of reference from which a client can answer the question (for example, "Are you male or female?"), within which frames there is a known range of possible responses and within which range there are clearly defined choices to represent the position of each client to situations in which a question (for example, "How shall we begin?") is used because the client has not yet begun to formulate an idea and needs to be led through the process of recall, organization, and evaluation of his or her experiences in order to do so. This is the range of questions on the closed-to-open continuum. Closed questions are like a kind of efficient, small-bore ammunition used to hit a target that is clearly in sight and not complex. On the other hand, open questions are used to pursue less well-defined issues requiring greater range, spread, and fire power. Between these two points there are intermediate steps where open responses within a more narrowly constricted range are appropriate (for example, "What is your earliest recollection as a child?" or "How are you feeling at this moment?").

Even when we are speaking of open versus closed questions, there is still a range of limits posed by each. These limits include control of the frame of reference, control of the time frame, and even control of the background data supplied. As you can see, the use of questions in counseling is a complex skill that deserves a great deal of attention in counselor training.

Ivey (1971) has suggested that questions are useful in counseling to help begin an interview, to help the client elaborate on a point of discussion, to help elicit examples of specific behavior, and to help focus the client's attention. To this list we add that questions are useful in developing client motivation to communicate and in directing the client toward the objectives established for the counseling interaction. In other words, questions are useful not only in facilitating self-exploration and self-understanding, but also in developing a relationship and leading the counseling process to a fruitful conclusion.

The ability to formulate good questions necessitates having specific objectives in mind beforehand. Effective questions are formulated only after adequate attention has been paid to specific objectives, and this has made questions risky for some counselors. If, for example, you use a question as an open invitation for the client to talk, you have to first be aware that what you want is for dialogue to begin and for the client to begin it. With this objective in mind, you ask "How would you like to begin?" instead of saying "Start talking!"

If you want specific information, you must tell this to the client. For example, if your client has talked at great length about his mother and completely failed to mention his father, you may feel that there is some significance in this omission. A facilitative question can be asked to clear up the concern while focusing the client's attention on the issue. You should state both the background of and the objective for the question.

Ms. Ramirez: You have talked at length about your mother and never mentioned your father. Is there some significance to this that I missed?

Questions find their way into counseling interactions whether we like it or not. The success of the counseling interaction depends on the quality of questions the counselor asks as well as on the quality of his or her reflective responses. Skillfully worded questions do a great deal to motivate the client to respond, because they serve as open invitations to talk and because they guide the client along more productive paths of interaction.

It is very important that the language used in counseling conform to the shared vocabulary of client and counselor. Moreover, vocabulary and syntax should offer maximum opportunity for complete and accurate communication of ideas between client and counselor. When the client is narrating and the counselor is reflecting, the counselor is, in a sense, checking out shared vocabulary and syntax to make certain that what is heard is what was meant.

When asking questions, we assume that the client shares the meaning, vocabulary, and syntax of our question in formulating a reply. Counselors do not usually check out the client's understanding of their questions before analyzing replies. Yet we know that each individual interprets spoken or written communication from a unique experience and personal viewpoint. Everyone who receives a communication understands and interpets the information according to personal, relevant past experiences. Providing a context out of experience is what gives meaning to the communication.

Our clients are often so overwhelmed by their own immediate needs that their replies to our questions must be interpreted in relation to these needs. This does not mean that we should avoid asking questions; rather, it suggests we use caution in interpreting the client's reply. A skilled counselor will check out the client's understanding of any complex question before interpreting the client's answer.

When dealing with the reflective response, the task of understanding is with the counselor. Reflective responding is the end point of a somewhat passive counseling activity. Asking questions is a much more active process. A question must be worded so that it ties into the respondent's level of information in a meaningful way. The counselor must make realistic assumptions about the client's knowledge and willingness to reply or take the risk that the client cannot or will not reply. In other words, the counselor must make a series of judgments before asking a question. These include (1) determining the client's knowledge and experience relative to the subject, (2) being assured that the client will understand the language used and (3) knowing that the desired answer is psychologically available to the client. Furthermore, the counselor must make a judgment about the frame of reference in which the question is cast by either learning the client's frame of reference, indicating a specific frame, or selecting a common frame. These judgments become more important as the counselor pursues more specific information, and they usually must be made quickly. Open questions are less risky for the counselor, because the client makes more assumptions in formulating his or her reply then does the counselor in formulating the question. Closed questions, on the other hand, place the greater responsibility on the counselor. However, because each individual, upon receiving a communication, must understand and interpret the information in the light of his or her own experiences, both parties in the questioning process bear some part of the burden of assumption making. Once the counselor has posed a question, whether open or closed, he or she must continue to keep in mind the context in which the reply will be given.

The counselor must also know the level of risk he is willing to accept in formulating a question. The risk must be assessed on the basis of the counselor's sense of confidence and on analysis of the client's ability to respond. This risk factor will determine, in conjunction with the counselor's predetermined objectives for asking the question, whether an open or closed question posed in a direct or indirect way is more appropriate.

A final word of caution: self-disclosure and self-exploration are not inherently magical qualities. In order to have impact, the client must see them as relevant and meaningful. If the counselor facilitates irrelevant disclosure, or even disclosure seen by the client as irrelevant to his or her problem, the result may be counterproductive. With this in mind, questions should have a purpose which should be clear to the counselor and related to the client. Appropriate questions should rise from what has already been said, not from what the counselor would like the client to discuss.

3

The Inappropriate Use of Questions

Questioning has been greatly misused and overused by counselors. When misuse occurs, it is damaging to the ultimate effectiveness of the counselor as well as to the counselor/client relationship. Several writers (Gazda et al., 1977; Patterson, 1974) have commented on the negative effects of misused questions. The two biggest misuses of questions are related to the quantity and quality of questions.

THE INAPPROPRIATE QUANTITY OF QUESTIONS

All too frequently, counselors rely on questioning to carry the weight of the interview. This is especially true for beginning counselors. A common practice is to almost automatically ask a question whenever the interview comes to a silent period. Long (1975) found that over 40% of all counselor responses during the initial interview were in the form of questions. This is considerably high for the initial session and indicates a possible lack of understanding on the counselor's part for the appropriate use of questions.

When counselors are at a loss for something to say, their natural tendency is to ask a question. When this happens, the counselor devotes more energy to thinking up new questions than to listening to what is being said. This shifts the responsibility for discussing the problem from the client to the counselor. It should be remembered that the counselor does have the overall responsibility for the structuring of the counseling process; however, the responsibility for self-disclosure, self-exploration, and ultimately for problem resolution rests with the client. The counselor is only responsible for *facilitating* these objectives.

Many reasons can be offered to explain the overuse of questioning by counselors. One explanation is a lack of basic understanding of what the client is saying or a lack of basic verbal interaction skills and training to facilitate meaningful discussion. When counselors feel the need to ask too many questions during an interview, it is usually because they have not used open-ended questions.

Closed questions are often hypotheses about the client formulated by the counselor. The counselor seeks validation of these hypotheses in the form of closed questions. Rephrasing the question from direct to open ended will produce facilitative responses and greatly reduce the need for additional questions. The overall effect of using open-ended questions contributes to client self-disclosure and self-exploration. Any direct or closed question can be rephrased as open ended and should contribute to achieving the counselor's objectives. For example:

Direct: How often do you use drugs?
Open: Could you tell me about your use of drugs?
Direct: Do you get along with your roommate?
Open: Could you tell me about your relationship with your roommate?
Direct: Did that make you feel angry?
Open: How did it make you feel?

When too many questions are asked, most of them are probably inappropriate. Gazda et al. (1977) have summarized some of the problems of inappropriate questions. They include the following counterproductive effects:

1. *Creating Dependency.*   Direct or inappropriate questions place the client in a dependent role.

2. *Placing Responsibility on the Counselor.*   Responsibility for problem solving rests with the counselor and not with the client, where it belongs. This reduces the client's active involvement in solving the problem.

3. *Reducing Self-Exploration.*   The direct question or the overuse of questions will limit the client's self-exploration. The client's only task is to answer questions. The conversation is then under the sole direction and responsibility of the counselor.

4. *Producing Invalid Information.*   Direct questions are sometimes asked in such a way that clients can anticipate what answer they *should* give. When this happens, the counselor may not be receiving valid and reliable information from the client. A counselor who asks a client, "Has this experience (counseling) been valuable for you?" is structuring the question to influence the client's response.

Few clients would be totally candid if their counselor asked a question in this form. It would be more appropriate to reformulate the question to allow for open-ended responses—responses which would not be suggestive of the counselor's bias or expectations. When the counselor is obviously anticipating a given answer, it is likely that it will be given. A more effective question would be, "Could you tell me how you feel about what we've been doing?" or "What is it that you liked most and least about what we've been doing?"

Several additional limitations of questioning should be added to this list.

5. Generating Feelings of Defensiveness, Hostility, and Resentment on the Part of the Client. Turning counseling into an interrogation or "twenty-questions" game will greatly impede the development of any facilitative relationship. Sometimes the very quality of the questions themselves will make clients feel they have to justify or qualify their responses:

Why did you do that?
How could you do that?
Did you think you wouldn't get caught?
Why did you wait so long?

Questions such as these evoke feelings completely counterproductive to any sense of spontaneity and openness essential to the counseling process. When most of the counselor's responses begin with a barrage of "who," "what," "where," and "why," negative effects are almost certain.

6. Fostering Poor Helping Skills. One of the greatest threats of inappropriate questions is their potential to inhibit the effective use of other important verbal response styles such as reflections, clarifications, and summarizations. Ultimately, this creates a situation that will frustrate the goals of counseling and limit the productivity of the interview. It should be remembered that a skilled counselor uses a variety of verbal response styles to accomplish the objectives of self-disclosure and self-exploration. Questions are only one such style.

In sum, avoiding the overuse of questions is a difficult but necessary skill. Without careful self-monitoring of verbal interaction behaviors, the tendency is always present for beginning counselors to overuse and misuse questions.

THE INAPPROPRIATE QUALITY OF QUESTIONS

We have talked about the inappropriate *quantity* of questions. We will now direct our attention to a similar topic: the inappropriate *quality* of questions. Such questions, by their very nature, are generally considered ineffective for facilitative communication. A few of the more prominent types of questioning responses that counselors should avoid are presented below.

"Why" Questions

Counselors should generally avoid "why" questions. Only occasionally do they serve a useful purpose. "Why" questions have considerable underlying implications that the counselor may not have intended. They can seem like accusations made by the counselor. They require a justification or explanation by the client that, at times, may not be within the scope of his or her present knowledge. They immediately put the client on the defensive.

A "why" question, in a sense, is asked to determine causality, motivation, or intent. Often, because these dynamics are so complex, the exact reasons *why* cannot be determined. "Why" questions also seem to convey a counselor's value judgment. While this may be an implicit message, it still suggests that what the client did or said was wrong, bad, or inappropriate. For example, "Why did you tell her that?" suggests that the client's behavior was not what it should have been.

Obviously, the utility of "why" questions is doubtful and their effect counterproductive. They fail to communicate the facilitative condition of respect to the client, since they require the client to justify his or her behavior to the counselor.

Most questions that use *why* can be rephrased into a more facilitative form by the counselor. In many cases, the counselor is more interested in "how" or "what" the events were that surrounded the situation being discussed. Questions phrased with "what" or "how" require the client to relate or describe the situation. There is no inherent causality or motivation associated with the answer and, because these questions are descriptive rather than explanatory, a valid answer is within the scope of the client's knowledge.

Example 1
Why: Why did you pick a fight with Johnny at recess?
Better: What happened at recess with Johnny?

Example 2
Why: Why did you break our contract after we agreed to it?
Better: Could you tell me about what happened?

Example 3
Why: Why do you let yourself get into these uncomfortable situations?
Better: What do you see as the reasons for being in these situations?

Example 4
Why: Why do you persist with this behavior?
Better: What do you think causes you to continue doing these things?

Thus, rephrasing "why" questions into another form will facilitate the client's response and better accomplish the counselor's objective. No accusation is present in these reformulated questions and clients do not feel they are under any pressure to justify their behavior. If counselors carefully consider the reason and purpose of each question, asking the appropriate question in the most appropriate manner will not be a complicated task.

Multiple-Choice Questions

Multiple-choice questions occur when the counselor gives the client a question and several alternative answers. At first thought, these questions appear to be open ended, but they are really closed questions since the client is given a limited set of responses from which to reply, for example,

Mr. Ford: How did you feel—upset or angry?
Mrs. Dayton: What has happened since last week? Did you decide to go or stay home?
Ms. Leonard: When you noticed that you were making progress, did that make you feel excited, happy, or what?

The last question the counselor asked is a good one, except for providing a selection of possible answers at the end. Multiple-choice questions bias the client's answer. A better way to phrase questions like this is to delete the multiple choice alternatives and simply ask the question. Let the client answer in his or her own words, as an open-ended question.

Multiple Questions

Multiple questions occur where the counselor poses several questions all at the same time to the client. The questions may differ in quality and importance. The most common response in this situation is to select one of the questions and answer it. Usually a client will respond by choosing the least threatening question and answering it. This can become confusing and frustrating to both the client and counselor. For example,

Miss Rhodes: What do you think he was thinking about? Or for that matter, what was his mother or father thinking about and what did you do then?
Mr. Donski: What kinds of careers have you been considering? Did you go to the career day or see the placement people, or have you just felt like you didn't know where to start?

Some of these questions would be useful if taken alone, but asked simultaneously leave the client in a quandary over which to answer first.

A counselor who tries to solve the problem too soon or who fears that he or she may forget to ask a particular question will use this form of questioning. When it happens, it is usually a sign of inexperience or lack of counseling skill. One question at a time is the obvious remedy.

Rhetorical Questions

Rhetorical questions are not really questions. They don't require an answer and in many cases really have no answer, but are a way for the counselor to state a given belief or fact in the form of a question. For example:

Ms. Daniels: What is it about teachers and discipline today?
Mr. Hankey: How does one ever find out the truth?

Questions of this type do little to further self-exploration and generally bring the discussion to a close. Rhetorical questions are loaded with value judgments that become irritating to the client. They communicate neither facilitative understanding nor respect. They also have a tendency to elevate the discussion to a high level of abstractness by talking in vague generalities rather than specifics and thus are of little value to facilitating self-understanding. Questions of this nature provide the counselor with an audience to state his or her own beliefs. This is little help to the client and should be avoided.

Accusative Questions

The purpose of an accusative question is to accuse the speaker of specific acts rather than seek information or facilitate self-exploration. For example:

"What were you doing in the first place?"
"How could you be sure?"

Accusations of this form leave the client no recourse but defensiveness or counterhostility. They fail to communicate facilitative understanding or respect. Accusative questions are by their very nature highly threatening to the client and have no useful function. Of all the questioning types, they are the least facilitative and definitely have no place in the counseling process.

Explanatory Questions

An explanatory question describes the counselor's position on an issue rather than facilitating client self-disclosure. Like the accusative question, it does little to contribute to client self-exploration and communicates a lack of understanding and respect for the client. For example:

"Are you aware that I feel uneasy talking to you about this subject, because of my position here?"
"Do you have any idea how many times I've had to deal with this problem?"

Questions of this type are not facilitative and should be formulated as responses other than questions. Specifically, explanatory questions shift the focus away from the client and his or her concern and redirect the interview towards the counselor's own special concerns.

4

Phase 1:
Exploration

Blocher (1966) considers counseling the process of helping an individual become aware of him- or herself and the ways of reacting to the behavioral influence of the environment. The primary role of counseling is to help the client establish personal meaning for his or her behavior and to develop and clarify goals and values for future behavior.

Within the process of counseling, the most important objectives include: (a) developing and maintaining a facilitative counseling relationship, (b) facilitating client self-exploration, (c) facilitating client self-understanding, and (d) integration of and working toward mutually agreed-upon goals. While many other objectives may be present, these are generally considered the most basic to all counseling approaches.

Most counselors would agree—and research has confirmed (Brammer, 1979; Delaney & Eisenberg, 1972; Egan, 1975; Rogers, 1951; Shertzer & Stone, 1980)—that the most important of all objectives is the establishment of a facilitative counseling relationship that will directly facilitate the goals of exploration, integration, and more constructive action. Communication in this relationship is based on respect, empathy, and congruence of the counselor and the client. These conditions should be present in all stages of the counseling process and are critical to the ultimate goals of counseling. Without the attainment of these core conditions, counseling will be ineffective (Egan, 1975; Truax, 1966).

The counselor's primary goal is to establish a facilitative relationship with the client. The counselor should communicate interest in the client and his or her communication, and should respond to the client communication with empathy, understanding, respect, and genuineness. The communication of these conditions should facilitate client self-exploration and disclosure. The client should begin to explore his or her experiences, thoughts, and feelings with the counselor, and the problem that brought the client into counseling should begin to unfold.

28

In this first phase of counseling, the counselor tries to help the client explore him- or herself as fully as possible using nonverbal and verbal interaction skills. The counselor should use only those verbal interaction skills that will facilitate the primary objective of the first stage of counseling. Trainees readily point to the importance of reflections, clarifications, and summarizations in communicating empathy, respect, and genuineness to the client. In addition, questions can also help establish a facilitative relationship and further client self-exploration and disclosure. Carefully constructed and appropriately utilized questions can communicate an understanding of and respect for the client and the genuiness of the counselor.

A closer examination of the core conditions should provide a better understanding of how the counselor's verbal behavior can foster these necessary conditions.

In 1961, Rogers outlined the conditions of empathic understanding, respect, and genuineness as necessary for a facilitative relationship. Considerable research has substantiated their necessity for constructive client change. *Empathic understanding* has received the most prominent attention in the counseling literature. Rogers (1975) offers this vivid definition of the concept:

> . . . entering the private conceptual world of the other and becoming thoroughly at home in it. It involves being sensitive, moment to moment, to the changing felt meanings which flow in this other person, to the fear or rage or tenderness or confusion or whatever, that he/she is expressing. It means temporarily living in his/her life, moving about in it delicately without making judgments, sensing meanings of which he/she is scarcely aware, but not trying to uncover feelings of which the person is totally unaware, since this would be too threatening. It includes communicating your sensings of his/her world as you look with fresh and unfrightened eyes at elements of which the individual is fearful [p. 4].

Quite similarly, Patterson (1973b) defined empathic understanding as the "understanding of another from an internal frame of reference achieved by putting oneself in the place of the other, so that one sees him and his world as closely as possible" (p. 20).

Respect is the acceptance without judgment or condemnation of another person as being worthy (Patterson, 1973). *Genuineness* refers to the counselor's ability to be real or honest with the client (Gazda et al., 1977). Both of these conditions are also prerequisites to facilitate the counseling relationship and contribute to meaningful client self-exploration and disclosure.

Not only must the counselor offer these conditions, but the client must recognize the extent to which they are offered if any degree of effectiveness is to be obtained. Emphasizing the importance of this distinction, Rogers (1961) has written that significant learning in counseling cannot occur unless the client perceives these conditions to exist. It is not sufficient that they are apparent to an outside observer; they must be communicated to the client. The mechanisms to facilitate the effective communication of these conditions are the verbal interaction skills of the counselor. While reflections and clarifications are the major forms of communicating these conditions, they are not the only ones. Questioning can also effectively communicate understanding, respect, and genuineness.

The appropriate use of questions can help enhance all three conditions. Facilitative questions communicate an interest in the client and his or her communication by demonstrating that the counselor is attending to the communication. Correctly formulated questions convey an understanding of the client and his or her world as it is communicated. Facilitative questions are sensitive to the thoughts and feelings of the client, and are directly related to the client's problem. In contrast, nonfacilitative questions are ineffective because they (1) redirect the focus of conversation to an irrelevant issue by changing the subject, (2) are overly threatening in their purpose, or (3) demonstrate a lack of understanding of the client. The nonfacilitative questioner becomes an interrogator, assuming an aggressive role that will endanger any relationship that has been established so far. Discrimination between appropriate and inappropriate questions becomes a critical and necessary skill for counselors to master. A clearer understanding of appropriate uses for questions can be achieved by illustrating some of the common types of questions employed in the first stage of counseling. The remainder of this chapter will provide the reader with the skills necessary to formulate questions that enhance the goals of the first stage of counseling—client self-exploration and disclosure.

TO HELP BEGIN THE INTERVIEW

The most difficult verbal responses for new counselors are those that begin the interview. When faced with a client whose expectations and level of cooperation are unknown, it is very difficult to be relaxed and spontaneous. Some clients are familiar with counseling and what it entails; most clients, however, are unaware of the counseling process and know very little about what to expect or what is expected of them. They are usually apprehensive and nervous during their introduction to counseling. A competent counselor must be able to deal with the client's apprehension immediately. Getting off to a good start is therefore crucial for effective helping.

There are several acceptable methods of beginning a counseling session. The counselor can remain silent, waiting for the client to take the initiative. An alternative is to structure the session by defining the purpose and limits of the interaction. Yet another alternative is to begin the interview with an open invitation to talk. All three of these methods place the major responsibility to talk with the client, and the silent counselor places the entire responsibility with the client. The structuring counselor is helped by defining the purpose of counseling. The questioning counselor assumes the greatest responsibility by openly inviting the client to talk.

An appropriate question or two may be a real asset for starting the interview and counseling process. Ivey (1971) considers this use of questions to be open invitations to talk. When a client comes for counseling, he or she has some apparent reason for concern. The skilled counselor can effectively begin the interview by the appropriate use of questions. It should say to the client, "I am interested in you; share your concerns with me." It should allow the client the freedom to talk about whatever he or she chooses. This communicates respect to the client and an understanding of the problem. When inviting the client to talk, use an open-ended question.

Here are some examples of questions often used to begin the interview:

Could you tell me a little about yourself?

What is it that I can help you with?

Well, we've got 45 minutes, so could we use this time to see how I can help?

Well, why don't you start by talking about what's on your mind?

Read the following student statement and select the counselor question that best begins the interview.

John: Mrs. Jones sent me down to see you about fighting in her class.
Mrs. Taylor: A. Well, John, why were you fighting?
    ❋   B. Well, John, why don't you tell me a little about what happened?
           C. How do you feel about getting caught fighting?

If you chose A, go to page 34.
If you chose B, go to page 35.
If you chose C, go to page 36.

You chose A

Well, John, why were you fighting?

You were to pick a question that best begins the interview with this student. This is not it. A facilitative question would ask "what" or "how" rather than "why." It would encourage John to discuss his experiences, thoughts, and feelings openly and at his own pace with the counselor.

This is a "why" question. It discourages self-disclosure and will arouse defensiveness in John, forcing him to prematurely generate a reason for his behavior. It assumes that he was fighting and fails to build a base of respect and understanding.

Go back one page and try again.

You chose B

Well, John, why don't you tell me a little about what happened?

You chose the correct question. This is an open invitation to talk and is the best type of question with which to begin a counseling session. It allows the client to start wherever he wants and keeps the responsibility to talk with him. Although this question starts with the phrase "Why don't you," it actually asks what happened rather than "Why did you behave a certain way?"

Question A ("Well, John, why were you fighting?") was a "why" question, arousing defensiveness and asking John to justify his behavior. Question C ("How do you feel about getting caught fighting?") prematurely asks him to express his feelings and also assumes his guilt.

Congratulations. Advance to page 37.

You chose C

How do you feel about getting caught fighting?

You were to pick the question that best begins the interview with this client. A facilitative question would provide an open invitation to talk. It would encourage John to discuss his experiences, thoughts, and feelings openly and at his own pace with you.

This question communicates a lack of respect for John, since it assumes his guilt. It prematurely asks him about his feelings and for this reason may arouse defensiveness. It structures client talk. A better question would allow more freedom in the client response.

Go back to page 33 and try again.

Read the following statement and select the counselor question that best begins the interview.

Roberta: I really don't know why I'm here. I really don't have anything to say. I just came because my friend told me that it might help.
Counselor: A. What exactly did your friend tell you?
　　　　　　B. Well, would you tell me a little about yourself?
　　　　　　C. Why do you think you should come here?

If you chose A, go to page 38.
If you chose B, go to page 39.
If you chose C, go to page 40.

You chose A

What exactly did your friend tell you?

You were to pick the question that best begins the interview. This is not it. This is an irrelevant question that focuses on Roberta's friend rather than Roberta herself. This client is apprehensive about the counseling process and unsure where to begin. A question like this immediately focuses on specific information and might arouse negative feelings and encourage defensiveness. It might also lead her away from free expression of herself and the major problem at hand.

A good beginning question is an open invitation to talk. The purpose is to facilitate self-disclosure and to build a relationship of trust and openness. Look for a question that demonstrates the counselor's concern and interest in the client.

Go back one page and try again.

You chose B

Well, would you tell me a little about yourself?

This is the correct response. It is an open-ended question that is serving quite appropriately as an open invitation to talk. It will allow Roberta to talk about any aspect of herself that she chooses, in her own words. It is an excellent way to begin building an effective counseling relationship. It is nonthreatening and demonstrates the counselor's interest in the client.

Turn to page 41.

You chose C

Why do you think you should come here?

You were to pick the question that best begins the interview. This is not it. This is a "why" question and will create unnecessary defensiveness from the client. Roberta is obviously apprehensive and unsure about why she is talking to a counselor. She is uncertain whether she wants to share herself with the counselor and this question is magnifying her concern by being too aggressive. By trying to push a resistant client, you will have little success.

A better question would attempt to facilitate a good relationship with the client. It will demonstrate the counselor's interest and concern, yet give her the freedom to respond in her own manner. Look for an open invitation to talk.

Go back to page 37 and try again.

You are a counselor, sitting in your office. Stephen, a client who has an appointment, comes in and silently sits down. List five questions you might use to begin the interview.

1. _____

   _____

2. _____

   _____

3. _____

   _____

4. _____

   _____

5. _____

   _____

Go to the next page.

Possible invitations to talk include:

1. Is there anything I can do for you?

2. How would you like us to spend our time together today?

3. What would you like to talk about?

4. Is there something you want to talk about?

5. How might I be of some help?

Look at the five questions presented.

a. Which two focus on the client's need to talk?
b. Which two focus on the counselor's desire to help?
c. Which two assume helping is going to occur?
d. Which three do not assume helping is going to occur?

Notice that question 1 ("Is there anything I can do for you?") and question 5 ("How might I be of some help?") are very similar. Both communicate the desire to be helpful. However, in question 5, the counselor assumes he or she can be helpful and wants to know what to do; in question 1, the counselor asks the client whether he or she can be of help.

Notice that question 3 ("What would you like to talk about?") and question 4 ("Is there something you want to talk about?") are very similar. Both focus on the client's need to talk. The difference is that in question 3 the counselor assumes the client has something he or she would like to share, whereas question 4 asks whether there is something the client wants to share. In question 2, the counselor asks, "How would you like us to spend our time together today?"

OPEN-ENDED QUESTIONS

After the client has begun to express him- or herself, the counselor should be concerned with establishing and maintaining a facilitative manner. The responses of the counselor should communicate an understanding of the client and his or her problem. The questions asked should be related to the material presented by the client.

Good questions attempt to get the speaker to more fully explore the significant aspects of what has already been said. Appropriate questions should arise from what has already been stated, not from what the counselor would like the client to discuss. Facilitative questions help the counselor focus statements around the significant issues and thus communicate understanding to the client.

Example 1
John: . . . then I got the letter from my father—on the morning of my final exam!
Mrs. Young: John, when you received the letter, how did it make you feel?

Example 2
Filipe: . . . and after all that, she sends back my ring!
Mr. Moreno: Wow! What was going on in your mind then?

In both these examples the counselor is posing a question that is intended to promote further meaningful and relevant self-exploration and disclosure.

Example 3
John: . . . so I finally opened the letter and it was just what I expected.
Ms. Roth: John, can't you see your father's reasons for writing that letter?

Example 4
Clara: . . . well, I wanted to find out more about different majors since I'm not doing too good in chemistry.
Mr. Cochran: Is that your only reason for coming to the counseling center?

It is apparent in both these examples that the counselor is not listening to what the client is saying. The counselor demonstrates this by asking questions that are not relevant to the client's previous response. These nonfacilitative questions communicate a lack of understanding to the client. Frequent use of questions like these is a common practice among beginning counselors. Not only are they damaging to the counseling relationship, since they communicate a lack of understanding and respect, but they inhibit effective helping.

Another criterion of a facilitative question is that it requires more than a one- or two-word answer. Questions that allow the client a choice of response communicate the counselor's respect of the client's right to determine the direction of the interaction. The purpose of a facilitative question is to get the speaker to disclose more information about a specific aspect of him- or herself or experiences. Closed questions, which require only a brief factual response or a "yes" or "no" answer, solicit a limited number of possible responses and do not prompt the speaker to talk. The most likely response to a closed question is to supply the one-word response required and then wait for the next question. Look at the following closed questions and the limited number of possible responses available to the client.

Closed Questions	*Possible Responses*
1. Is this a new problem?	1. Yes, no
2. Do you think that counseling can help with this problem?	2. Yes, no
3. How long has this been happening?	3. (A time period—a day, a week, etc.)

On the other hand, open-ended questions prompt the speaker to reveal more information about him- or herself. The number of possible responses to an open-ended question is unlimited. It allows the speaker a freedom of response, which is impossible with a closed question. Although the response to an open-ended question will most likely be longer than the response to a closed question, it is also likely that the speaker will wait for the next question when the response has been completed to the question at hand. Since questioning establishes the listener as the "master of ceremonies" no matter what type of questions are used, questions should be used sparingly. When too many questions are asked, the speaker expects them and waits for them to direct the conversation. Although open-ended questions allow the speaker to influence the direction of the interaction, they still establish the listener as the person who controls the topic and the depth of exploration.

Look at the following open questions and the wide number of possible responses available to the client.

Open Questions	*Possible Responses*
What is your mother like?	1. My mother is a beautiful woman who always likes to look nice.
	2. My mother is someone who thinks a lot about men and pleasing them.
	3. My mother is very depressed a lot of the time.
	(The client could discuss any of an indefinite number of mother characteristics.)
How did you feel when your friends ignored you?	1. It hurt me deeply.
	2. I was very upset.
	3. I could have killed her.
	(The client could discuss any number of emotions.)

Study the following stimulus and responses. Notice the difference between the open and closed responses as they apply to the same client statement.

Glenn: Steve's into drugs. He really doesn't have his head on straight. I really don't know what to do.

Closed Questions
1. Which Steve?
2. Has Steve ever dropped acid?

Open Questions
>   3. What does Steve do that tells you he doesn't have his head on straight?
>   4. How does Steve's being into drugs affect you?

The key difference between open and closed questions lies in the structure of the question. Open questions allow a wide variety of responses. Closed questions limit the client's responses. Because of this difference, they also differ in their communication of respect. Open questions convey respect to the client. They communicate acceptance of the client as a person and demonstrate trust in the client to determine, within limits, what is appropriate and inappropriate to the problem. They further demonstrate respect by allowing the client to talk about the problem in his or her own words. Closed questions, on the other hand, have a tendency to evoke the counterproductive feelings of defensiveness, hostility, and frustration. Additionally, they negate further client exploration by bringing the discussion to a close.

Here is an example of the use of closed questions in trying to begin an interview.

Mrs. Ricardo: Hello, Bob, I'm Mrs. Ricardo, your counselor.
Bob: Hi.
Mrs. Ricardo: Did you want to see me?
Bob: Well, oh, I guess so.
Mrs. Ricardo: Okay, then, what's on your mind?
. .
Then I take it you're serious about transferring?
Bob: Yes, I think so.
Mrs. Ricardo: Is this something you've been thinking about for a while?
Bob: Uh huh.

This is an example of how open questions could be used to start the same interview.

Mrs. Ricardo: Hello, Bob, I'm Mrs. Ricardo, your counselor.
Bob: Hi.
Mrs. Ricardo: Well, what is it that we can do for you?
Bob: Well, I don't like this school . . . and I wanted to transfer to another college.
Mrs. Ricardo: Okay, well, could you tell me a little more about your decision?

In this example, the open-ended question facilitates further discussion and exploration, whereas the closed question requires more questions, thus leading to an interrogation. Ideally, the counselor's questions should be designed to facilitate clarification of what has been said. They should allow the client the freedom to share his or her problem in his or her own words.

The dangers of using closed questions during initial counseling sessions are considerable. For one, they require the counselor to ask too many questions. The counselor might concentrate on what to ask next and might not listen to what is being said. Secondly, beginning the counseling relationship with a series of closed questions could inappropriately define the counselor/client relationship, by establishing fixed roles for each participant. The counselor becomes the question-asker and the client the question-answerer. Once this pattern is established, it becomes very difficult to alter. The counselor's role then becomes one of generating an unending list of questions for the client to answer. With a framework such as this, the client may assume that sooner or later enough questions will be asked and the problem will be solved! In addition, this type of response pattern does little to encourage self-understanding. It is difficult for the counselor to convey any degree of empathic understanding or respect for the client when the predominant response is a continuing list of inappropriate questions.

The third danger is the over-dependence of counselors on questions. This commonly occurs when counselors generate questions because they cannot think of anything else to say during an interview. Questions asked for this purpose tend to be closed questions.

The use of open-ended questions will overcome these dangers. They allow the client to talk and the counselor to listen. As Gazda et al. (1977) point out, the open-ended question elicits spontaneous self-disclosure, whereas the closed question deprives clients of the opportunity to express themselves and their problems in their own words. Thus, open-ended questions are always more facilitative than closed questions.

Given the following statement by a high school student, which of the following teacher questions is open ended?

Hal: Sometimes nothing seems to go my way. Today on my way to school not only did I lose the heel off my shoe but I lost my homework.

Professor Brown: A. Which class's homework did you lose?

B. Did you ever have a day like this before?

C. How do you feel when nothing seems to go your way?

If you chose A, go to page 48.
If you chose B, go to page 49.
If you chose C, go to page 50.

You chose A

Which class's homework did you lose?

You were to pick the example of an open-ended question. This is not it. This is a closed question, since the range of possible responses is greatly limited. The student can respond to this question by naming the course or courses for which he lost his homework. This question does not encourage him to reveal a great deal of information about himself. Most likely, Hal will respond by naming a course and then wait for the next teacher question.

An open-ended question would encourage a student to reveal information about himself. The range of possible responses would not be limited to a predictable set. Freedom of response is the key difference between open and closed questions. Questions that require "yes" or "no" answers are examples of closed questions.

Go back to page 47 and choose the open question.

You chose B

>*Did you ever have a day like this before?*

You were to pick the example of an open-ended question. This is not it. This is a closed question, since the range of possible responses is greatly limited and requires only a "yes" or "no" answer. At most, Hal could respond, "Yes, way back in November I had a day that was almost as bad."

An open-ended question would encourage the student to reveal more information about himself. The range of possible responses would not be limited to a predictable set of responses. An open-ended question usually does not solicit short, concise answers. The key difference between open and closed questions is the freedom of response allowed. If there is only one correct response or if the number of possible responses is greatly limited, the question is closed.

Go back to page 47 and choose the open question.

You chose C

How do you feel when nothing seems to go your way?

This is an open question. There is no predefined list of responses from which the student must choose. He is free to describe his feelings in as much or as little detail as he likes. This question encourages him to reveal more information about how he feels when nothing seems to go his way.

The other alternatives limit Hal in the type of response he is free to make. Question A calls for him to name the courses for which he lost his homework. Question B requires a "yes" or "no" answer. Both of these questions put limits on the type and length of the student responses.

Perhaps comparing response questions to test questions will prove helpful in explaining the difference between open and closed questions. Multiple choice, true/false, and matching are all examples of closed questions. The student has a limited number of responses from which to choose. Arithmetic problems, where the student is required to add, subtract, multiply, or divide a pair of numbers, are closed questions since there is only one acceptable response. Essay questions are open questions, since the freedom of response and the number of acceptable responses is diverse.

Advance to page 51.

Read the following statement by a high school student. Which of the following counselor questions is an example of a closed question?

Marc: I've had to share a room with my kid brother ever since he was born. My sister gets to have a room all to herself. I'm being treated unfairly again . . . as usual.

Mrs. Hamlin: A. In what other situations do you think your parents treat you unfairly?

B. How many sisters do you have?

C. Why do you feel so mistreated at home?

If you chose A, go to page 52.
If you chose B, go to page 53.
If you chose C, go to page 54.

You chose A

> *In what other situations do you think your parents treat you unfairly?*

You were to pick the example of a closed question. This is not it. The above question is an open-ended question. An open-ended question allows the speaker a greater range of acceptable responses. In response to the above question, Marc could describe one or several incidents in as much or as little detail as he chooses.

In response to a closed question the speaker must respond from a predetermined list of acceptable answers. "Yes" or "no" questions are closed questions, since the speaker must respond from a set of two responses—"yes" or "no." Closed questions inhibit interaction, since the student merely answers the question and then waits for the next question to be directed to him.

Go back to page 51 and try again to choose the closed question.

You chose B

How many sisters do you have?

You picked the correct response: this is a closed question. It limits various aspects of the response. The above question limits the type of response to a numerical answer. It further limits the response in that it calls for a specific fact for which there is only one correct response. Marc's response to this question will most likely be to say a number and then wait for the next question from Mrs. Hamlin. Obviously this type of question will not encourage Marc to talk more openly about himself.

The two alternative questions—"In what other situations do you think your parents treat you unfairly?" and "Why do you feel so mistreated at home?"—allow for more extended responses and a greater freedom or response style.

Proceed to page 55.

You chose C

Why do you feel so mistreated at home?

You were to pick the example of a closed question. This is not it. The above question is an open-ended question that allows the student a greater range of acceptable responses. In response to the above question, Marc could describe why he feels so mistreated at home as well as his reaction to the situation. The question does not greatly limit the nature or length of his response. Open-ended questions, like the one above, allow the responder greater freedom of expression.

Closed questions limit the freedom of expression of the responder and limit the length of the acceptable response. A closed question would inhibit interaction, since Marc would merely answer the question and then wait for the next question to be directed toward him. Even questions that allow a greater range of acceptable responses can be poor questions; however, the above "why" question can put the client off and in effect close down his desire to respond at all.

Go back to page 51. Try again to choose the closed question.

　　　Many closed questions can be restated as open questions. Rewrite the following closed questions as open questions.

Stacey: I'm really afraid to go home today. When my mother sees my
　　　report card she'll be mad.
Closed Question
　　　Are you afraid of her yelling at you?
Open Question

_____

_____

Closed Question
　　　Did you flunk any courses?
Open Question

_____

_____

Go to the next page.

Following are possible open-ended responses.

Stacey: I'm really afraid to go home today. When my mother sees my
report card she'll be mad.
Closed Question
Are you afraid of her yelling at you?
Open Question

What are you afraid of?
_____

Closed Question
Did you flunk any courses?
Open Question

What is it about your report card that your mother would dislike?
_____

Go to the next page.

Rewrite the following closed questions as open questions:

Tana: I feel fenced in. I want to move to a warmer climate, but I'm afraid I won't find a job. I like all my friends here, but for some reason I'm just not satisfied in this area.

Closed Question
Do you think you'd be happier in another part of the country?
Open Question

_____

_____

Closed Question
Do you have any idea what it is about this area that dissatisfies you?
Open Question

_____

_____

Go to the next page.

Following are possible open-ended responses.

Tana: I feel fenced in. I want to move to a warmer climate, but I'm afraid I won't find a job. I like all my friends here, but for some reason I'm just not satisfied in this area.

Closed Question

Do you think you'd be happier in another part of the country?

Open Question

What makes you think you'd be happier in another part of the country?

Closed Question

Do you have any idea what it is about this area that dissatisfies you?

Open Question

What is it about this area that dissatisfies you?

Go to the next page.

QUESTION ORIENTATION

Before formulating a question, the counselor must decide to what aspect of the answer he is going to respond. The counselor has a choice of responding to the experience the speaker presents, to his or her thoughts about the experience, to his or her feelings about his experience, or to any combination of the three.

The *experience component* of a message is defined as those incidents the speaker reports, describes, or has experienced. The *cognitive component* of a message is the speaker's thoughts, including thoughts about something as concrete as an experience or as abstract as an idea. The *affective component* of a message includes the client's feelings. It includes such emotions as anger, joy, depression, frustration, disappointment, and hostility.

A message can contain at most three component parts. The first describes an incident or some other external material, such as the content of a novel or the thoughts of someone aside from the speaker. It answers the question, "What happened?" The second component contains the speaker's cognitive reaction to what happened. It tells what the person thinks about it. These are thought of as one unit and are called the *content of the message*. The third part of the message contains the speaker's "gut reaction" to the experience. It provides the speaker's feelings about what happened and is the *affective component* of the message.

Some messages do not have all three components. Messages like "I don't like my father" and "I feel terrific" have only affective or feeling components. Statements like "I left home last night" or "I'm going out tonight" are largely free from feeling and only express observable events. A facilitative question is directed toward material already mentioned by the speaker, as opposed to being directed toward new or tangential material. Facilitative questions related to the content already expressed by the speaker are often termed *content-related questions.* They attempt to get the speaker to explore the significant content more deeply or to supply missing information to increase the listener's understanding of the material. A *feeling-related question* is directed at feelings already mentioned by the speaker. A *facilitative question* can also ask the speaker to define feelings thus far only implied. Most messages contain both content and affective components. The speaker must decide to respond to one or the other or both.

Go to the next page.

Let's look at an example:

Peter: I'm concerned about my son. He's not doing as well in school as I think he should. He used to like school; now he acts reluctant to go.

The listener can formulate either a *content-related* question—"What makes you think your son isn't doing as well in school as he should?"— or an *affect-related* question—"How does your son's school performance make you feel?"—or clarification of both the *affective and the content components* of the message—"What performance would be necessary by your son for you to feel less concerned?"

Most people think they can differentiate cognition from affect, but it is something few people have ever learned. The expression "I feel" is often used to precede thoughts: "I feel Bill is doing a good job" and "I feel this is too hard for me." Both statements would be better preceded by "I think" or "I judge" because they represent thoughts rather than feelings. Feelings are taken more seriously than thoughts: to get others to listen more carefully, people try to call feelings what are really thoughts. At times people are afraid to express feelings but think others expect them to, so they attempt to meet the expectation by game playing—giving thoughts and calling them feelings. Whatever the reason, it is something that must be unlearned. The reverse of this phenomenon seldom occurs. How often do you hear someone say "I think mad" or "I think disappointed"?

Advance to page 61.

In summary, there are three possible component parts of a message. Any message can have one, two, or all three of them.

1. What happened?
   a. The speaker's experience
   b. Description of an external event
   c. An observable incident, written material, or the thoughts and feelings of another person
   d. The experiential component
2. What do you think about what happened?
   a. The speaker's thoughts
   b. The speaker's cognitive or mental reaction to experiential components
   c. The cognitive component or cognitive content
3. How do you feel about what happened; what is your cognitive reaction to what happened?
   a. The speaker's feelings
   b. All "gut-level" reactions
   c. The affective component

Parts 1 and 2 combined compose what is defined as the *content or theme of the message.*

Turn to page 62.

Let's examine a stimulus statement and break it down into its three component parts.

Martha: At times I don't know what to do. My husband and I argue constantly. I'd like things to be better.

Part 1: What happened? (the experiential component)

My husband and I argue constantly.

Part 2: What does the speaker think about what happened? (the cognitive component)

At times I don't know what to do. I'd like things to be better.

Part 3: How does the speaker feel about what happened? (the affective component)

None

Notice that Martha did not tell us her affective reaction to the incident. She only told us what happened and what she thought about it. Parts 1 and 2 comprise the content or theme of the message and are responded to together.

Advance to page 63.

Let's examine another stimulus and delineate its component parts.

Juanita: Kathy's my friend, but if I tell her I'm going back to school, she'll be jealous. I'm afraid she won't want to talk to me.

Part 1: What happened? (the experiential component)

> *Stated:* Kathy's my friend.
> ___
> *Implied:* Juanita is going back to school. Kathy would like to go
> back to school.
> ___

Part 2: What does the speaker think about what happened? (the cognitive component)

> But if I tell her I'm going back to school, she'll be jealous. She won't
> want to talk to me.
> ___

Part 3: How does the speaker feel about what happened? (the affective reaction)

> I'm afraid.
> ___

Notice that part of the experience component of the statement is implied. We can infer from what is stated that Juanita is going back to school and that Kathy would like to go back to school. Juanita fears jealousy by a close friend. The message is a projection of a possible future event and the fear associated with that event. Juanita fears Kathy's jealousy and the loss of her friendship.

Go on to page 65.

   Read the following stimulus statement and formulate the following *open questions.*

Juanita: Kathy's my friend, but if I tell her I'm going back to school she'll be jealous. I'm afraid she won't want to talk to me.

Experientially oriented question

_____

_____

Cognitively oriented question

_____

_____

Affectively oriented question

_____

_____

Go to the next page.

Following are sample questions that focus on the various aspects of the stimulus statement.

Juanita: Kathy's my friend, but if I tell her I'm going back to school, she'll be jealous. I'm afraid she won't want to talk to me.

Experientially oriented question

What prompted your decision to go back to school?

Cognitively oriented question

Aside from not talking to you, how else might she express her jealousy?

Affectively oriented question

How would you feel if Kathy didn't talk to you?

Go to the next page.

Read the following statement. Break down this statement into its three component parts.

William: Sometimes nothing seems to go my way. Today on the way to
    work, not only did I run out of gas, but I lost the belt off my coat.
What is the external message? (In other words, what happened?)

_____

_____

_____

What is William's cognitive reaction to this situation?

_____

_____

_____

How does William feel about what happened?

_____

_____

_____

Go to page 68.

If you have advanced to this page without filling in the blanks with the correct responses, you may have trouble completing the rest of this program!

Here is the correct response.

William: Sometimes nothing seems to go my way. Today on the way to work, not only did I run out of gas, but I lost the belt off my coat.

Experience

Today on the way to work, not only did I run out of gas, but I lost the belt off my coat.

Thoughts

Sometimes nothing seems to go my way.

Affect

None overtly expressed.

Go to page 69.

Read the following statement. Break it into its three component parts.

Carlos: My wife makes me the same breakfast every morning: eggs and sausage. Every day I tell her I hate sausage. It's so frustrating. I'd rather make my own breakfast.

What happened? What is the external message?

_____

_____

_____

What does Carlos think about this situation?

_____

_____

_____

How does Carlos feel about what happened?

_____

_____

_____

Go to page 70.

Here is the correct response.

Carlos: My wife makes me the same breakfast every morning: eggs and sausage. Every day I tell her I hate sausage. It's so frustrating. I'd rather make my own breakfast.
What happened?

My wife makes me the same breakfast every morning: eggs and

sausage. Every day I tell her I hate sausage.

What does Carlos think about this situation?

I'd rather make my own breakfast.

How does Carlos feel about what happened?

It's so frustrating.

Notice that the phrase "I hate sausage" was classified as an experience component rather than an affective component, since it is a statement about a past event. The statement "I'd rather make my own breakfast" is classified as a cognitive statement since Carlos thinks he'd prefer to do his own cooking rather than be served something he doesn't like.

Try page 71.

Read this stimulus statement and formulate the following open questions.

Leslie: Work is such a drag. If I didn't have so many debts, I'd quit. I don't even want to go in the mornings. I just can't wait til I retire.

Experientially oriented question

———————————————————————————

———————————————————————————

Cognitively oriented question

———————————————————————————

———————————————————————————

Affectively oriented question

———————————————————————————

———————————————————————————

Go to the next page.

Read the following stimulus statement and formulate the following open questions.

Leslie: Work is such a drag. If I didn't have so many debts, I'd quit. I
   don't even want to go in the mornings. I can't wait til I retire.
Experientially oriented question

Why don't you tell me more about your work?
_____

Cognitively oriented question

Besides financial reasons, are there any other reasons why you
_____
don't quit?
_____

Affectively oriented question

How do you feel about retiring?
_____

Go to the next page.

THE FACILITATIVE QUESTION

A facilitative question shows the client that the counselor is actively listening; that is, attending to the client's communication. It conveys counselor understanding and should be directly relevant to the client's problem. A facilitative question is asked for a specific purpose and adds meaning to the counselor/client interaction process. It is an open-ended question related to either the content or the client's feelings. It is also related to information already discussed by the client and highlights the major problem at hand. A good facilitative question solicits missing information or clarifies previously encountered material. It can help start an interview or clarify client behavior. A facilitative question communicates understanding and respect. Most importantly, it helps the client better understand him- or herself. Keeping these things in mind, which of the following counselor questions is the most helpful?

Terry: I'm really depressed about the way things are going at home between me and one of my sisters. It's never been like this before. We don't get along at all. It seems like the least little things just get us going at each other.

Mr. Martinez: A. How do you get along with your other sisters?

B. Which sister is it that you are having trouble with?

C. What type of things get you "going at each other"?

If you chose A, go to page 74.
If you chose B, go to page 75.
If you chose C, go to page 76.

You chose A

How do you get along with your other sisters?

You were to choose the most helpful question. This is not it. This question shifts attention away from the major problem at hand to a secondary issue. Terry is concerned about her relationship with one of her sisters; drawing her attention to her relationship with her other sisters serves no purpose at this time. In other words, this is not a content/feeling-related question, since Terry did not mention her relationship with her other sisters.

However, this question has several good points. It is open and actively seeks more information.

Turn back one page and try again.

You chose B

Which sister is it that you are having trouble with?

You were to pick out the example of the most helpful question. This is not it. Although this question seeks more information about the problem at hand, it is not the most helpful. This is a closed question and the information it seeks is of trivial importance.

Turn back to page 73 and try again.

You chose C

What types of things get you going at each other?

You chose the correct response; this is the most helpful question. It seeks specific information about why Terry is having trouble with her sister. It is an open-ended question, and therefore allows Terry freedom of response. It is directly related to the content she already described. It seeks clarification of the sentence, "It seems like the least little things just get us going at each other." It asks, in a sense, "namely, what little things?"

Turn to page 77.

Given the following stimulus, which of the counselor questions is the most helpful?

Roy: My brother called last night. The one who's in the Army. He is not going to come home for Christmas. I really wanted to see him. And besides, I already bought him a present.

Nina: A. Do you have any other brothers in the Army?

B. How do you feel knowing he's not going to be coming home?

C. What do you want to do with the present you bought him?

If you chose A, go to page 78.
If you chose B, go to page 79.
If you chose C, go to page 80.

You chose A

Do you have any other brothers in the Army?

This response is irrelevant to the problem at hand. Roy misses his brother, who is in the Army. It does not matter whether this is his only brother or whether he has ten other brothers in the Army. The fact is that he misses this brother.

Turn back to page 77 and try again.

You chose B

How do you feel knowing he's not going to be coming home?

Of the three response options, this is the most helpful. It is a feeling-related question.

The question above asks Roy to describe how he feels about the problem at hand. It allows him great freedom in expressing himself.

Roy has implied that his brother is not coming home for Christmas. This question recognizes this, and asks him to express how he feels about it.

Turn to page 81.

You chose C

What do you want to do with the present you bought him?

You were to choose the most helpful question. This is not it. This is a content-related question. It is directed at helping Roy decide what he is doing to do with the present. The issue of the present is a secondary problem in this stimulus. The primary problem is the fact that Roy misses his brother. A feeling-related question would be more helpful.

Turn back to page 77 and choose the best question.

Read the following stimulus. Which of the following counselor questions is most helpful?

Vinnie: Ted doesn't have his head on straight. He's into drugs. I can't relate to him at all anymore. I thought maybe you could talk to him.

Lauren: A. What type of drugs is Ted into?
          B. In what ways are you having trouble relating to Ted?
          C. Is Ted having trouble with his school work because of this problem?

If you chose A, go to page 82.
If you chose B, go to page 83.
If you chose C, go to page 84.

You chose A

What type of drugs is Ted into?

You were to choose the most helpful question. This is not it; it is a content-related question. It seeks clarification of the term "drugs" from Vinnie. It is a closed question, since the number of possible responses are limited. A more helpful question would facilitate interaction by providing the opportunity for a diverse number of responses.

Go back to page 81 and choose another answer.

You chose B

In what ways are you having trouble relating to Ted?

This is a content-related question, since it seeks clarification of information previously presented by Vinnie. The counselor is soliciting specific samples of how Vinnie is having trouble relating to Ted. This is an attempt to obtain clarification of the generalization, "I can't relate to him at all anymore."

This question is the most helpful since it focuses on Vinnie's relationship with Ted, rather than exclusively on Ted and his drug problem. The question communicates to the speaker, "I am interested in you and your concerns."

Go to page 85.

You chose C

Is Ted having trouble with his school work because of this problem?

This is not the most helpful response. This is a closed question. It requires a "yes" or "no" answer. It gives Vinnie the job of verifying or nullifying the listener's projections about the problem. Lauren is guessing that Ted's problem with drugs affects his school work. She is asking Vinnie if this projection is true instead of allowing him to express the problem himself.

This question stirs Vinnie away from the major problem expressed. The relevancy of this question depends on whether or not Ted is having problems with his school work. Instead of guessing at likely problems, Lauren should try to get Vinnie to clarify problems already expressed.

Go back to page 81 and choose another answer.

SUMMARY

Counseling is a verbal and nonverbal interaction process that includes the following basic objectives: (a) developing and maintaining a facilitative counseling relationship, (b) facilitating client self-exploration, (c) facilitating client self-understanding, and (d) integration and working toward mutually agreed-upon goals.

Facilitative questions—as well as the other verbal interaction skills of reflection, clarification, and summarization—can help the counselor achieve the basic objectives in the counseling process.

The effective use of questions can contribute to the core conditions of empathic understanding, respect, and genuineness.

Nonfacilitative questions generally prove ineffective because they can: (a) change the focus or topic of discussion to irrelevant issues, (b) be overly threatening in their purpose, or (c) demonstrate a lack of understanding for the client.

Questioning during the exploration phase of counseling can be used to help begin the interview, to help the client explore meaningful and relevant issues, and to aid in appropriate client self-disclosure. Questions used for these purposes generally employ open-ended rather than closed questions.

Questions can be directed toward any of the three possible components of the client's message: the experiential, the cognitive, or the affective components. The expert counselor can direct his or her questioning to the most relevant component or components.

The counselor's evaluation of the client's verbal interaction can greatly improve the effective use of questioning, which will in turn help achieve the basic objectives of counseling.

Appropriate questioning is an important adjunct to the counselor's verbal and nonverbal repertoire, and thus greatly enchances the basic objectives of the exploration phase of the counseling process.

EVALUATION

Judging its effectiveness—evaluating—our use of questions is a continuing process across the entire counseling experience. For questions to be effective in their purpose during this phase of counseling, the counselor must evaluate his or her efforts both as each session is proceeding and again after each session.

This type of ongoing evaluation requires answering a simple question: was the purpose of each question achieved? The answer to this question must come from an examination of what the client said, how it was said, verbal and nonverbal behaviors and actions of the client, and an overall inquiry into these issues as a result of the dialogue that was produced by each verbal interaction effort of the counselor.

This type of immediate evaluation is always difficult because, as Okun (1976) points out, the counselor does not always have obvious observable criteria. However, the counselor must be aware of the basic purposes for each question as well as the overall purpose of this phase of counseling: to facilitate exploration of the client problem or concern. With this in mind, continuous attention to what happens during the interview will provide an indication of the effectiveness of each effort.

It has been emphasized that all verbal interaction techniques should be used for specific purposes: to inquire, to stimulate, to expand, to clarify, to understand, and to enhance further exploration. This necessity of purpose is even more acute with the use of questions. It is this type of evaluation which will ultimately determine whether the counselor's use of questions was facilitative or not. Receiving answers to each question is *not* alone sufficient criterium to conclude their facilitation in this phase of counseling. An example should demonstrate this point quite clearly.

Lily: Well, I'm not sure which of the two majors to go into and I have to decide by the end of the week.

Ms. Wright: What were the two majors?

Lily: Well, it was either going to be psychology or philosophy.

Ms. Wright: Don't they overlap a bit?

Lily: Not really. I'm interested in animal behavior in psychology and in philosophy my main interest is the ancient philosophers.

Ms. Wright: Then you wouldn't be interested in combining both areas in some way—or would you?

Lily: Well, I don't see how that would be feasible. I mean, I don't think I could. It would be like having two majors.

Ms. Wright: How difficult would it be to have two majors? Could you take extra courses?

Lily: I don't know how many extra courses I'd need to take or what good it would do me for graduate school.

Ms. Wright: Which graduate schools were you thinking about?

In this example, the counselor had a purpose in each question: to obtain information. Additionally, the counselor did receive answers to each question that provided information previously unknown. Many of the questions were open ended. However, the questions were *not* facilitative to exploration primarily because they neglected the point of the client's concern: making a decision between two equally attractive goals and the urgency of such a decision. Answers to these questions alone were not adequate criteria for evaluating both their appropriateness and their effectiveness.

What, then, is? To answer this question, the counselor must ask him- or herself the following evaluation questions while the interview proceeds and again after it has finished. If the answer is "yes" to most of these questions, then the counselor's use of questions was appropriate. If the answer is "no" to most of these evaluation questions, then some changes in his or her verbal interaction skills are necessary.

QUESTIONING RESPONSE CHECKLIST: PHASE 1

1. Was there a purpose to each of the questions?
   yes   no   n/a

2. Did the answers provided by the client provide new information? Did they clarify, expand, and/or enhance further exploration?
   yes   no   n/a

3. Did the questions keep the client on the topic under discussion?
   yes   no   n/a

4. Could the questions used have been better worded as reflections, clarifications, or direct statements?
   yes   no   n/a

5. Were most questions asked as open-ended questions?
   yes   no   n/a

6. Did the client respond to open-ended questions with additional responses that facilitated exploration?
   yes   no   n/a

7. Has the use of questions helped the client explore issues and concerns not previously discussed?
   yes   no   n/a

8. Were questions appropriately timed and placed in the interview so that the client did not feel interrogated?
   yes   no   n/a

9. Did the client seem overly threatened by any questions?
   yes   no   n/a

10. Did the client's nonverbal behaviors indicate a favorable response to the questions asked?
    yes   no   n/a

11. Did the client demonstrate any verbal or nonverbal behaviors to indicate that he or she felt understood by the counselor?
    yes   no   n/a

12. Were appropriate affective components of client responses covered by the questions?
    yes   no   n/a

13. Were appropriate experiential components of client responses covered by the questions?
    yes   no   n/a

14. Were appropriate cognitive components of client responses covered by the questions?
    yes   no   n/a

15. Was the session begun by an open invitation to talk?
    yes   no   n/a

16. Did the client respond positively to open invitations to talk?
    yes   no   n/a

17. Was there sufficient self-exploration of the client's concern to proceed to the next phase of the counseling process?
    yes   no   n/a

Asking yourself questions similar to these, both during and after the interview, will help you begin monitoring what you ask and why you're asking it, as well as give some feedback from the client as to its value. This continuous monitoring or evaluating will greatly facilitate the overall objectives in the exploration phase of counseling.

Phase 2:
Integration

During the first phase of counseling, the objectives of the counselor are to establish a facilitative relationship with the client and to help the client explore him- or herself as fully as possible. The counselor's responses contain high levels of respect and empathy. In Phase 1, the counselor finds out as much as possible about the client, and the client learns to trust and communicate openly with the counselor. When the client has expressed the problem as fully as possible and seeks direction and input from the counselor, it is time to move to the second phase of helping.

During Phase 2, the counselor helps the client better understand him- or herself, his or her world, and the difficulties being experienced. The counselor not only communicates with respect and understanding, but also analyzes the information obtained and seeks the expansion and clarification of relevant ideas. In this phase the counselor actively focuses on the client's implied and underlying communication and attempts to integrate this with his or her understanding of the client. In accomplishing this goal of increased client understanding, questions can be appropriately used in several ways.

In this phase, questions can be used by the counselor to seek clarification of unclear terms and to seek specific examples of generalizations presented by the client. Questions can also be used to focus the client's attention to an important aspect of a present communication or redirect attention to an important aspect of a previous communication. Finally, questions can be used by the counselor to confront the client with discrepancies between various aspects of his or her communication. This chapter discusses these uses of questions and contains training in the skills involved.

CLARIFYING QUESTIONS

The primary function of clarifying questions is to help the counselor better understand the client. Counselors use them to clarify the client's communication—to obtain missing information or better understand information already presented.

Clarifying questions can also help the client better understand him- or herself and the nature of his or her communication. They help the clients express themselves more freely and better evaluate their situations.

Use 1: To Obtain Factual Information

The purpose of the first type of clarifying question is to help the counselor obtain information not already presented by the client. The counselor may be interested in facts about the client or the client's experiences, or the counselor may be seeking more personal information from the client about thoughts and feelings. The counselor may also be seeking information from the client relative to the client-counselor relationship. In all of these cases, questions are used to obtain information from the client not already presented.

The most common use of questions in daily communication—and the most overused and misused in counseling—is to obtain specific factual information. Most counselors have had a good deal of training and experience with asking questions, and do so with ease. The most universally asked questions—How many children do you have? Where do you work? How do you like the weather?—contribute little to the counseling relationship and should be excluded from the counseling interview. Before a counselor asks a question about specific factual or experiential information, he or she should counsider: Do I really need to know this information to better understand the client or am I just asking this question out of curiosity or to keep the discussion going? If reflection points to an inappropriate reason, the counselor is both wasting counseling time and also conveying a lack of respect and genuineness to the client—both of which are counterproductive to effective helping.

There are times when specific information is needed from the client, which has been intentionally or unintentionally omitted. In this case, using open-ended questions may not be appropriate. A direct question asked to obtain specific information is more effective.

Example 1
Anne: I feel like I work all day and never have time for myself.
Ms. Lopez: What hours do you work?

Example 2
Julie: I can't afford to buy all my sisters birthday presents.
Mr. Marcos: How many sisters do you have?

In these examples, the client is omitting information relevant to the problem conveyed. Because of this vagueness, the counselor's questions were designed to obtain missing information and thus clarify the communication. However, in neither of the above examples is the client information essential. Counselors should remember that clients' perceptions are just as important as the situations they actually find themselves in.

Direct questions attempt to obtain the needed information in the most expeditious manner. However, questions of this type should always have a legitimate purpose that is directly relevant to the client's situation.

Questions seeking to obtain factual information should be used with caution, because they have the potential danger of becoming overused and nonfacilitative. The negative effects of overuse parallel those noted earlier for closed questions. Their appropriateness depends more on timing and purpose than on the content of the questions.

Use 2: To Provide Specific Examples of Generalizations

There are times when client responses are vague and abstract. The client will speak in a general sense rather than from a personal viewpoint. Clarifying questions can encourage the speaker to offer specific examples of previously stated generalizations. They help the listener get concrete examples from the speaker.

Concrete communication from the client is desired in the second stage of counseling. The client who is willing to share ideas about problems in specific detail is easier to help than the client who talks in generalities. Asking questions to clarify and elaborate an idea can be very useful in resolving vagueness and making the abstract more concrete.

Example 1
Leona: My husband and I get into fights just about anything. Most things we fight about seem so trivial afterwards.
Miss Donner: Can you give me an example of something you had a fight about?

Example 2
Austin: My brother bothers me whenever I try to study.
Mr. Michaels: In what ways does he bother you?

In both of these examples the counselor asks the client to clarify general statements by providing specific examples. This serves several functions. First, it helps the counselor better understand the client. Second, it communicates to the client that it is important to be concrete. Third, the specific examples the client gives either affirm or deny the generalizations offered earlier. This will provide the client with a stronger reality base.

Read the following client statement. Which of the counselor questions ask the client to clarify some portion of the original statement by providing a concrete example?

Eric: I really don't like my brother. When I'm around him, I wonder how he and I could be from the same family. He's nice, and other people sure like him, but somehow he seems to lack a sense of integrity or something.

Mrs. Judd: A. How do you feel about the other members of your family?
B. What does he do that seems to illustrate a lack of integrity?
C. What do other people see in him that they like?

If you chose A, go to page 94.
If you chose B, go to page 95.
If you chose C, go to page 96.

You chose A

How do you feel about the other members of your family?

You were to pick a question that requests clarification of some portion of the original stimulus. This is not it. A clarifying question would ask Eric to define his vague vocabulary, supply missing information, or give a specific example of a generalization.

Question A *redirects* Eric. It asks him about the rest of his family, which he has not mentioned. He has only expressed concern about his relationship with his brother. It is this relationship that needs clarification.

Turn back one page and try again.

You chose B

What does he do that seems to illustrate a lack of integrity?

This is the correct response. It seeks clarification of the phrase "lack a sense of integrity." This is a key phrase for both Eric and Mrs. Judd to better understand Eric's thoughts. Did you notice that question A ("How do you feel about other members of your family?") directs the speaker away from the original problem content? Question C ("What do other people see in him that they like?") asks Eric a question he can't answer; he can only describe the world from his own frame of reference.

Turn to page 97.

You chose C

What do other people see in him that they like?

You were to choose a question that requests clarification of some portion of the original statement. This is not it. A clarifying question would ask the speaker to define unclear vocabulary, supply missing information, or provide a specific example of a generalization. At a quick glance, question C seems to seek clarification of the statement "other people sure like him." Close examination shows that Eric is unable to answer this question; he can only speak from his own experience and about his own reactions to his brother. He does not know what it is that other people like about his brother.

Turn back to page 93 and try again.

Read the following stimulus statement. Underline the phrases that need further clarification and then write two questions that ask the client to clarify unclear phrases by providing specific examples of generalizations.

Antoinette Jones: I'm really angry at my boss. He always puts me in positions that are unfair. Most times I don't know what to do. If I don't listen to him he'll punish me again, and if I do, I feel like I'm letting myself down.

1. _____

_____

_____

2. _____

_____

_____

Go to the next page.

I'm really angry at my boss. He always *puts me in positions that are unfair.* Most times I don't know what to do. If I don't listen to him *he'll punish me again,* and if I do, I feel like I'm letting myself down.

Possible Clarifying Questions

1. Can you give me a specific example of a position your boss has put you in that was unfair?

2. How did your boss react the last time you failed to follow his wishes?

Go to the next page.

Use 3: To Clarify Unclear Terms

A third type of clarifying question asks the clients to clarify unclear terms—to expand or elaborate upon what has already been expressed. This type of question asks the client to define terms and feelings which, although previously expressed, were vague and unclear. This type of question does not solicit specific examples from the client but rather clarifies unclear information.

This type of question prevents misunderstandings from occurring between the counselor and client. Clients often assume that counselors understand the intent of their vocabulary and modes of expression. Counselors should not make this assumption but rather should use clarifying questions to encourage the client to expand on expressions that seem unclear. Skilled counselors know when they *assume* they understand their clients rather than really *understanding* them. Questions help clarify these assumptions.

Example 1
Liza: I'm going to leave my husband. I'm tired of putting up with his antics.
Fred: What do you mean by "leave your husband"?

Example 2
Daniel: I'm dissatisfied with my sex life. My wife and I hardly ever make love.
Elaine: Can you tell me what you mean by "hardly ever"?

In both of these examples the counselor could have assumed she or he understood the client's communication; instead, the counselor in the first example knew "leave" could mean anything from "file for divorce or separation" to "go away for the weekend." Instead of trying to guess what the client meant, the counselor *asked.* Similarly, the counselor in the second example asked the client what was meant by "hardly ever," since it could mean anything from "once a week" to "once a year."

Given the following statement, which of the listener questions seeks clarification of previously presented information?

Elizabeth: My husband and I had another fight last night. I'm afraid to go home. He's so mad at me I think he'll do something crazy.

Martin: A. Nothing will happen. Why don't you go home?

B. Do you have these fights often?

C. You said he'll do something crazy. What do you mean by crazy?

If you chose A, go to page 102.
If you chose B, go to page 103.
If you chose C, go to page 104.

You chose A

Nothing will happen. Why don't you go home?

You were to choose an example of a clarifying question. This is not it. Clarifying questions ask the speaker to define terms, supply missing information, or supply specific examples of generalizations. They request that the speaker expand and clarify some previously stated information. Question A doesn't really ask a question. It says, "Go home. Nothing will happen." It also says, "There's no reason for you not to go home." It does not ask Elizabeth to explain her problem further, but rather ignores the problem. Clarifying questions are designed to help the listener better understand what the speaker said.

Go back one page and try to choose the correct response.

You chose B

Do you have these fights often?

You were to choose an example of a clarifying question. This is not it. A clarifying question asks the speaker to define terms, supply missing information, or supply specific examples of generalizations. It requests that the speaker expand and clarify some previously stated information. The clarifying question is designed to help the listener better understand what the speaker said.

Question B seeks missing information. The listener, Martin, seeks more information concerning Elizabeth's marriage in general. A clarifying question would try to help Martin better understand Elizabeth's fear and the fight she just had with her husband.

Go back to page 101 and try again.

You chose C

> *You said he'll do something crazy. What do you mean by crazy?*

This is the correct question. It requests Elizabeth to define the term "crazy." Its aim is to ascertain why Elizabeth is afraid of her husband and to find out what she thinks he'll do.

Did you notice that question A ("Nothing will happen. Why don't you go home?") doesn't really ask a question but rather provides advice? It discounts Elizabeth's fear and tells her she has no reason not to go home. Question B seeks missing information; however, the information sought is not specific to the situation described but rather to the marriage in general.

Advance one page.

Clarifying unclear terms also entails the clarification of feelings stated or alluded to by the client.

Feelings are critical to self-disclosure and self-exploration, and questioning can facilitate their open discussion. This use of questions is especially important for clients who have difficulty expressing or expanding on their feelings.

Example 1
Monica: He didn't even read my paper. He just put a C on it.
Rachel: How did that make you feel?

Example 2
Curt: I felt upset.
Roland: What do you mean by "upset"?

In the first example, the client is expressing strong feelings but has not identified their nature. They could be anger, hostility, hurt, sorrow, or others important to self-exploration and self-understanding. The counselor is using questions to help the client identify and clarify the feelings that are present. In the second example, the counselor is asking the client to clarify the term "upset," so that he can better understand what the client means by this expression.

Caution is advised in these efforts, since it may be threatening to the client to press for concreteness or specificity too early in the counseling process (Carkhuff & Berenson, 1977; Eisenberg & Delaney, 1977). Only after a good relationship has been established can raising questions that require more concreteness facilitate the goals of self-disclosure and self-exploration.

Before asking a clarifying question, the counselor must determine which words or phrases of the client stimulus require clarification. Read the following stimulus statements and underline those phrases that require further clarification.

Christopher: I really feel close to you. No one has given me as much help and support. I wish we would have met under other circumstances. Things might have been different then.

Kimberly: I am afraid of my own anger. At times I feel like I'm boiling up inside. Sometimes the littlest thing can cause me to blow up at those closest to me.

Turn to the next page.

Christopher: I really feel close to you. No one has given me as much help and support. I wish we would have met under other circumstances. *Things might have been different then.*

Kimberly: I am afraid of my own anger. At times I feel like I'm boiling up inside. Sometimes *the littlest thing can cause me to blow up* at those closest to me.

In Christopher's statement, he is projecting the counselor/client relationship into other settings. The phrase "things might have been different" is the key to understanding how Christopher would like to define his relationship with the counselor. A valuable question would be, "How might things have been different?"

With Kimberly, the phrase "the littlest thing can cause me to blow up" is critical to understanding her. The manner in which she expresses her anger and what provokes it remain undefined. A question like, "What about your anger frightens you?" might prove facilitative.

Advance to the next page.

Read the following stimulus statements and underline those words or phrases that require further clarification.

Missy: It's getting harder and harder to come in here. A lot of things that happen here are upsetting. I can't get your negative qualities out of my mind.

Candy: I'm embarrassed to invite my friends over when both my parents are home. The things they do in the kitchen you wouldn't believe.

Turn to the next page.

Missy: It's getting harder and harder to come in here. *A lot of things* that happen here are *upsetting.* I can't get your *negative qualities* out of my mind.

Candy: I'm embarrassed to invite my friends over when both my parents are home. *The things they do in the kitchen* you wouldn't believe.

In Missy's statement, reference to "upsetting things" and "negative qualities" both require clarification. Initially the counselor should focus on what is upsetting her, perhaps by asking, "What happens that is upsetting to you?" The negative qualities Missy referred to are probably only one of several factors contributing to her upset. Since reference to upset focuses on client affect and allows for a greater freedom of client response, it is the preferred response.

In Candy's statement, it is necessary to find out what she finds embarrassing as well as what her parents do in the kitchen. The "embarrassing" part is the preferred avenue of exploration, since it focuses on client affect, allows for a greater freedom of response, and is less threatening. Questioning Candy directly concerning parent behavior might promote embarrassment and defensiveness.

Advance to the next page.

Read the following client statements. Underline the words that need further clarification. What are possible questions you might ask these clients?

Helen: I'm really scared. At times my mother acts crazy. I wonder if she's going to hurt me if I misbehave. At times I feel like doing something drastic.

Clarifying Questions

_____

_____

_____

James: I'm worried about my wife. I know she's having a serious problem but every time I try to get her to talk about it she's hostile.

Clarifying Questions

_____

_____

_____

Go to the next page.

Helen: I'm really *scared.* At times my mother acts *crazy.* I wonder if she's going to *hurt me* if I misbehave. At times I feel like doing something *drastic.*
Possible Questions

What do you mean by "drastic"? When you say "crazy," what do you mean? In what way do you feel scared?

James: I'm worried about my wife. I know she's having a serious problem but every time I try to get her to talk about it she's *hostile.*
Possible Questions

Could you tell me more about feeling worried? What type of problem is your wife having? What do you mean by "hostile"?

Go to the next page.

Respond to this client with questions that clarify her feelings. The client is a 35-year-old mother of three children, recently separated from her husband.

Well, then he just left. He always said he'd just be gone someday, and now he is. I don't know what to do. I'm at the end of my rope. I wish this had never happened to me.

1. _____

   _____

2. _____

   _____

3. _____

   _____

Go to the next page.

Possible Clarifying Questions

1. Could you tell me how this makes you feel?

2. What kinds of feelings are you experiencing?

3. This situation seems to provoke strong feelings in you; could you perhaps describe them for me?

    The counselor questions are asked to help the client clarify her feelings about her situation. While she does not specifically mention any feelings in her response, many feelings are no doubt present. The use of clarifying questions will help her understand a critical area of the counselor/client interaction—the exploration of feelings. This area will be important for developing the appropriate degree of self-awareness necessary for effective helping.

Go to the next page.

FOCUSING QUESTIONS

Many clients will overwhelm their counselors with a considerable amount of information concerning several problems they are experiencing. When given the opportunity to openly discuss their problems with a nonjudgmental counselor, they often dscuss everything about their situation.

The counselor can help the client sort out what is relevant from what is irrelevant and focus on a particular issue or feeling that is central to the problem's resolution. Clients do not always see the critical aspects of a situation in the same perspective as do counselors. By using focusing questions, the counselor can see the major problem and begin effective helping.

A focusing question is an open question that tries to narrow the topic of conversation while allowing the client freedom of response.

When a counselor perceives one present focus as too broad, she or he may suggest that the client select an appropriate focus—one more manageable or narrow in scope.

In the first type of focusing question, the focus is selected by the client; in the second, the counselor decides which issues are important and selects one. Notice that, in response to the following client statement, either type of focusing response could be used.

Joanne: I'm having so much trouble I don't know where to begin. My sister's in the hospital and I have to visit her. My children are mad at me for not spending enough time with them. And on top of it all, my boss put me on probation for getting behind in my workload. I don't know what to do.

Counselor A: Of all the things you've mentioned, which one seems to be the most troublesome?
Counselor B: Why don't we talk about what's happening at work?

Notice that Counselor A gives a greater amount of freedom and responsibility to the client. Counselor B, on the other hand, selects a specific area for the client to consider.

When a client has difficulty focusing, it is up to the counselor to help. The counselor should focus the client's attention on a specific problem only when one problem clearly emerges as the most important. Important problems will be continually mentioned by the client and/or related to other problems mentioned. If it has been difficult in the past for the client to focus on a specific problem, guide his or her attention. If there is no clear problem or if you don't have enough information, let the client select the focus of the interaction.

Read the following statement by a 35-year-old client. Which of the counselor questions asks him to focus his previous statement?

Clyde: I don't know what to say. My little girl broke her arm and then my wife left me for no apparent reason . . . oh, and another thing, I can't seem to find any place to live and my lease expires in two months.

Mr. Wong: A. Wow! Is there anything else that's happened? Have you had any problems with your other children, and is this daughter all right?

B. Do you feel that when one thing goes wrong everything goes wrong?

C. Clyde, could we go back to the part about your wife leaving? Is that a good place to start?

If you chose A, go to page 118.
If you chose B, go to page 119.
If you chose C, go to page 120.

You chose A

> *Wow! Is there anything else that's happened? Have you had any problems with your other children, and is this daughter all right?*

You were to choose an example of a question that asked Clyde to focus or redirect his previous statements. This is not it. A focusing question would narrow the range of topics for Clyde to discuss, and help him determine an appropriate topic to pursue.

Question A is really a set of three questions. Even without evaluating each of the individual questions, it's possible to say that this form of questioning is not facilitative. This series of options does not add to the client's focus, but rather complicates his lack of focus. Clients who have a problem focusing are further confused by a series of questions, since they add the counselor's questions to their own list of problems. In responding to a series of questions, a client will usually choose the least threatening question.

Go back to page 117 and try again.

You chose B

> *Do you feel that when one thing goes wrong everything goes wrong?*

You were to pick an example of a question that asks Clyde to focus his previous statement. This is not it. A focusing question would communicate interest in a specific topic. It would help him choose—or would choose for him—a specific experience that warrants further discussion.

Question B is a rhetorical question. It doesn't really ask a question, but rather states presumed client feelings. It doesn't promote client disclosure or concreteness, but rather prompts the client to confirm the counselor's hypothesis. It doesn't help the client focus on a specific aspect of his problem, but rather treats the problem globally.

Go back to page 117 and try again.

You chose C

> *Clyde, could we go back to the part about your wife leaving? Is that a good place to start?*

This is the correct response. It is a good example of a question designed to focus Clyde's attention to one of the more serious concerns. It helps him focus his thoughts and words on a specific problem and tries to prevent him from rambling off on irrelevant tangents.

Did you notice that question A ("Wow! is there anything else that's happened? Have you had any problems with your other children, and is this daughter all right?") is really three distinct questions? Or that question B ("Do you feel that when one thing goes wrong everything goes wrong?") is really the counselor's hypothesis concerning Clyde's feelings? Both questions contribute to the client's lack of focus rather than condense the problem to manageable form.

Go to the next page.

Linda, a 35-year-old client, begins the interview with the following statement. Which of the counselor questions is the most helpful?

Linda: Everything seems to be going wrong. I'm in graduate school and I hate it. I'm not doing well and at times I wonder what's the point. My family wants me to stay home and care for them but when I do I just don't feel satisfied. But I don't like working either. Teaching school isn't always fun but I don't know what else to do.

Larry: A. I can see you have a lot of things bothering you. What seems to be of most concern?

    B. How does the conflict between your behavior and your family's desires make you feel?

    C. Maybe you could tell me a little bit about your job situation.

If you chose A, turn to page 122.
If you chose B, turn to page 123.
If you chose C, turn to page 124.

You chose A

I can see you have a lot of things bothering you. What seems to be of most concern?

This is the most helpful question. It allows the client the freedom to choose the areas of greatest concern. It places the responsibility of future content interaction with Linda. Since it is early in the counseling process and there is no clear major problem, it seems best to allow the client the choice of what's most important to her. The counselor has very little information on which to base a judgment, and is therefore safe to let the client select a topic for discussion.

Notice that question B ("How does the conflict between your behavior and your family's desires make you feel?") prematurely focuses on feelings; question C ("Maybe you could tell me a little bit about your job situation.") prematurely judges the significance of each problem.

Go to the next page.

You chose B

> *How does the conflict between your behavior and your family's desires make you feel?*

This is not the most helpful question. It focuses on the client's feelings. It asks Linda to share her feelings as they relate to one specific problem. Larry, the counselor, could have asked her to focus on her feelings surrounding any one of the problems mentioned. Asking her to discuss her feelings after only one statement seems premature. A better question would first have her focus on a specific problem and explore it more fully.

Turn back to page 121 and choose the most helpful question.

You chose C

Maybe you could tell me a little bit about your job situation.

This is not the best question. It asks the client to focus her attention on one of several problems mentioned. However, at this early stage in the helping process, no single problem has emerged as the most critical. Therefore, based on Larry's knowledge about Linda and the manner in which she has presented her problems, it seems premature to select a problem for her to focus on.

Turn back to page 121 and choose the best response.

REDIRECTING QUESTIONS

At times during the counseling process, it may be necessary for the counselor to have the client discuss material related to factual content or feelings that were discussed earlier in the interview or in a previous interview. In this case, the counselor may wish to use redirecting questions to guide the client back to this material. Redirecting questions can also be useful when clients discuss issues that appear to be unrelated or tangential to the problem. Clients tend to use these tangents to avoid talking about sensitive issues or they may feel these issues are relevant to their problem.

A redirecting question, posed in an open-ended form, may help the client attend to the topic of discussion. Examples of redirecting questions are:

Earlier you mentioned your feelings about failing the course, and I was wondering if we could go back to that for a second.

Could we talk a little bit about something you mentioned earlier: your reaction to his feelings?

The use of questions to facilitate focus and redirection implies an active and direct role by the counselor in structuring the course of the interview. This is necessary at certain times in the counseling process (Eisenberg & Delaney, 1977). Generally, in the early phase of counseling when the overall objective is to develop an effective counseling relationship and facilitate client disclosure, less direct structuring will be required. But later, in Phase 2, when problem identification and understanding are occurring, the amount of direct structuring will by necessity be greater. The exact degree of responsibility the counselor assumes for providing structure and direction in the interview depends on the counselor's personal style and theoretical orientation. Nonetheless, there will be numerous occasions when focus and direction will be required to further the goals of the various phases of the counseling process.

Read the following client statement and pick the counselor response that asks the client to redirect his thinking.

Jonathan: I've felt so depressed for weeks now. All the hassles at home haven't helped it any either. My wife's been on me for weeks because I don't do anything with her. I just want to sleep whenever I'm at home. The kids are upset because I don't take them anywhere. Everyone's hassling me. Sometimes, I really just want to get away from it all . . . .

David: A. It sounds like you're having a difficult time. Do you really think you could get away from all of this?

B. Why do you suppose this seems to be all happening now?

C. It sounds like many of your problems are related to the depression you're experiencing. Could you tell me about it, starting at the very beginning?

If you chose A, go to page 128.
If you chose B, go to page 129.
If you chose C, go to page 130.

You chose A

> *It sounds like you're having a difficult time. Do you really think you could get away from all of this?*

You were to choose an example of a question that asks the client to redirect the flow of the interview. This is not it. The first part of this response is a reflection of Jonathan's difficult situation. It communicates to him that David, the counselor, has heard his problem, but it inappropriately ignores Jonathan's feelings of depression. The second part of this response is a rhetorical question that has little relevance to the client's problem. The issue of getting away or being able to get away will do little to facilitate client self-understanding and will contribute little to further meaningful self-disclosure.

The purpose of redirecting is to help the client focus on the important issue of the problem before he gets side-tracked on other concerns. A better response would recognize the client's emotions and try to help him center his disclosure around the major issue at hand.

Go back one page and choose the correct response.

You chose B

Why do you suppose this seems to be all happening now?

You were to choose a question that asked the client to redirect the flow of the interview back to the major problem at hand. This is not it.

This response asks a "why" question that is premature for the client's present state of self-understanding. "Why" questions often presume responsibility and impose guilt. They have little value in prompting further self-disclosure and awareness. "Why" questions are better left unasked, especially at this point in the counseling process.

A better response would deal with client affect. It would help Jonathan focus on the major source of difficulty and allow him the freedom to discuss his problem in his own words.

Go back to page 127 and try again.

You chose C

> *It sounds like many of your problems are related to the depression you're experiencing. Could you tell me about it, starting at the very beginning?*

This is the correct response. David, the counselor, is redirecting the client to the most important concern mentioned in his response—his depression. When many problems are presented all at once, it is easy for counselors and clients to wander far afield. The redirecting question prevents this from happening by redirecting the dialogue to the issue that will best facilitate continued self-disclosure and contribute to the client's self-awareness.

Did you notice that response A ("It sounds like you're having a difficult time. Do you really think you could get away from all of this?") reflects the client's experience but ignores his depression? It also asks him a rhetorical question that will promote not client disclosure but rather client defensiveness? Did you notice that response B ("Why do you suppose this seems to be all happening now?") is a "why" question and implies client responsibility? This question will promote defensiveness and reduce meaningful client self-disclosure.

Advance one page.

Alfred is a 17-year-old client on probation for auto theft. Write three questions that a counselor would use to redirect the client's discourse.

Well, my parents really don't care about what happens to me. They never have, even when I was a little kid. I could do whatever I wanted to. What about those cops who busted me? Did they tell you about how they beat me up just because I wouldn't go over to their police car with them?

1. _____

2. _____

3. _____

Go to the next page.

Examples of redirecting questions

1. Could you tell me something more about your parents?

2. How did you feel when your parents didn't seem to be concerned about you?

3. Let's get back to your parents: how do they feel about this situation?

Example 1 is redirecting the client to the issue of his parents. This seems to be the most relevant to his current problem. The question will help him to get back to relevant information and avoid rambling on with other issues.

Example 2 is an effort to redirect the client to explore feelings that were implied earlier in the interview. Even though these feelings were not stated directly, they appear to be quite relevant to Alfred's situation. The counselor's question will redirect him to consider his feelings in this issue.

Example 3 is another effort by the counselor to redirect Alfred to talking about his parents and his perception of their feelings. This should help him avoid bringing up irrelevant issues and keep him focused on issues that seem relevant to the overall problem. Redirecting Alfred's thoughts would be more appropriate than addressing the issues he raised in the last part of his response, since they don't directly relate to the overall counseling goals.

CONFRONTING QUESTIONS

Confrontation is a very delicate and difficult skill for the beginning counselor to implement. Yet it is quite necessary for effective helping (Carkhuff & Berenson, 1977; Gazda et al., 1977). Confrontation is used when different aspects of the speaker's communication contradict each other. A confronting response points out and seeks clarification of these contradictions. For problem resolution or new behaviors to occur, the awareness and resolution of ambiguities is critical. Discrepancies exist for most people between what they say and what they do, as well as between their different thoughts and feelings.

Confronting these discrepancies provides the client with another avenue for self-exploration and possible resolution of the problem. It will also contribute to the counselor's understanding of inconsistencies and ambiguities in the client's behavior. Clients must be aware of their inconsistencies in order to gain self-understanding.

In some cases, confrontation by the counselor is the only way to facilitate awareness in the client. Most people do not like facing the unpleasant aspects of their behavior and so unconsciously resist any attempt by the counselor to focus on them. When this occurs, an appropriate confrontation will facilitate self-understanding.

Questions are one form of confronting. Asking questions can help point out and clarify contradictions between two verbal statements or between verbal and nonverbal behavior. Below are four examples of confronting questions:

1. "Earlier you stated you lost your homework. Then how could you have given it to Jane to copy when you got to school?"
2. "Why do you smile when you tell me how upsetting it was for you to flunk third grade?"
3. "How do you think you can resolve the discrepancy between what you think you should do and what you really want to do?"
4. "How do you account for these feelings in view of what you mentioned earlier?"

These examples demonstrate the more common uses of questions for confrontation. While it is difficult for most beginning counselors to develop facilitative confrontation skills, it is an essential part of effective counseling. Generally speaking, the use of confronting questions is most effective in the later phases of counseling as it becomes more necessary to develop specific goals for problem resolution (Eisenberg & Delaney, 1977).

Premature or inappropriate confrontation can have damaging side effects (Carkhuff & Berenson, 1977; Gazda et al., 1977). It can make the client defensive, hostile, or angry, and can contribute to the client's feeling of not being understood. Confrontation can communicate a lack of respect or trust for the client's thoughts and feelings, resulting in many cases in premature termination of the counseling process. Confrontation, therefore, is a serious endeavor. Whenever there is a sound basis for the counseling relationship, however, the potential positive effects of confrontation outweigh the possible negative effects.

When used appropriately, questions can have many beneficial functions for facilitative verbal interaction. Primarily, they demonstrate to the client that he or she is being attended to and understood. They also provide the counselor with necessary information and means of exploration of the problem. The skilled counselor uses questions effectively to attain his or her counseling objectives.

Read the following stimulus statement by a woman who is ending her relationship with a man she has lived with for four years. Choose the counselor response that is an example of a question that attempts to clarify apparent contradictions.

Janet: I wish Bruce would just leave. I've been working in the yard all day and all I can think about is the good times we've shared. He's done a lot of nice things for me during the past four years while we've lived together. Today I looked at the tree he planted and just started to cry.

Jack: A. Why do you want Bruce to leave?

    B. There seem to be a lot of positive aspects to your relationship, yet you want Bruce to leave. Can you explain?

    C. What are some other things Bruce has done that you like?

If you chose A, go to page 136.
If you chose B, go to page 137.
If you chose C, go to page 138.

You chose A

Why do you want Bruce to leave?

You were to choose an example of a question that clarifies apparent contradictions. This is not it. Such a question would try to clarify two statements Janet made or a statement she made and her nonverbal communication. Question A asks her to clarify the statement "I wish Bruce would just leave." It is an open-ended question since it does not structure or limit her response. Janet is free to provide behavioral or cognitive reasons for her decision. The question focuses on the present situation. It seeks justification of a decision that seems inconsistent with the rest of the statement. Nonetheless, this is a valuable question even though it didn't specifically highlight apparent contradictions.

Go back to page 135 and try again.

You chose B

> *There seem to be a lot of positive aspects to your relationship, yet you want Bruce to leave. Can you explain?*

This is the correct response. The purpose of this question is to point out and seek clarification of the apparent contradictions in the client statement. Janet says she wants Bruce to leave, yet she demonstrates very positive caring for him. She talks about the things she likes about him and even reports crying when thinking of him. Did you notice that question A ("Why do you want Bruce to leave?") asks her to clarify the statement "I wish Bruce would just leave"?

This is an open-ended question. The reasons Janet gives can be behavioral or affective. Question C ("What are some other things Bruce has done that you like?") asks her to clarify the statement "He's done a lot of nice things for me during the past four years while we've lived together." Notice that this question ignores her present situation and feelings and instead focuses on past events.

Go to page 139.

You chose C

What are some other things Bruce has done that you like?

You were to choose an example of a question that clarifies apparent contradictions. This is not it. Such a statement would seek clarification between two statements made by the speaker.

Question C seeks clarification of the statement "He's done a lot of nice things for me during the past four years." It asks the speaker to be more specific in her description of the positive events that have occurred during the four years. It is an open-ended question. It ignores Janet's present situation and feelings and instead focuses on past events. This question neither illustrates nor focuses on any contradictions in Janet's statement.

Go back to page 135 and try again.

Given the following statement by a high school student, which of the following counselor responses is an example of a question that asks the student to clarify apparent contradictions?

Brian: School is a bummer. Nothing I learn here is good for anything. Sometimes I feel like I'm just wasting my time. Maybe I should just quit.

Mrs. Ward: A. You feel like school's a waste of time, yet you still come. Why?

B. Is it because several of your friends have quit that you want to quit?

C. Do your parents want you to get a job?

If you chose A, go to page 140.
If you chose B, go to page 141.
If you chose C, go to page 142.

You chose A

You feel like school's a waste of time, yet you still come. Why?

This is the content-related question. The purpose of this question is to point out and seek clarification of the obvious contradiction between the student stimulus and his overt behavior. Brian says he wants to quit school, yet he keeps attending.

Did you notice that question B ("Is it because several of your friends have quit that you want to quit?") and question C ("Do your parents want you to get a job?") both seek verification of the counselor's hunch? In both of these responses, Mrs. Ward is guessing at why Brian wants to quit school. In neither case is the question related to the original student stimulus, since Brian did not mention his parents or his friends. Also notice that both of these are closed questions and require only a "yes" or "no" answer and would not facilitate student disclosure.

Turn to page 143.

You chose B

Is it because several of your friends have quit that you want to quit?

You were to choose the question that sought clarification of contradictions. This is not it. Such a question would seek clarification
between two statements made by the speaker, or between the speaker's
statement and his behavior.

Question B is not directly related to the original student statement.
Brian did not mention that several of his friends have quit. In this
response, the counselor is guessing at the cause of Brian's dissatisfaction. Mrs. Ward has proposed her theory in the form of a closed question. Brian now has to verify or nullify her theory, with a "yes" or "no"
answer. A facilitative question would help him realize and express the
reason for his dissatisfaction with school—not propose theories as to its
cause.

Turn back to page 139 and choose the correct response.

You chose C

Do your parents want you to get a job?

You were to choose the example of a question that sought clarification of contradictions. This is not it. Such a question would seek clarification between two statements made by the speaker or between the speaker's statement and his behavior.

Question C is not directly related to the original student stimulus. Brian neither mentioned his parents nor indicated in any way that his parents were persuading him to quit school. In this response, the counselor is guessing at the cause of Brian's dissatisfaction. Mrs. Ward has proposed her theory in the form of a closed question. Brian must now confirm or reject her theory verbally, by supplying a "yes" or "no" answer. A more helpful question would persuade Brian to examine what he thinks are the reasons for his dissatisfaction with school and solicit these reasons from him.

Turn back to page 139 and choose the correct response.

Joe is a 20-year-old college junior who is on academic probation. Read the following statement, then write two questions that will confront him on relevant discrepancies.

Well, it's really difficult for me to study. I have so much work. These courses really overload you. You'd think there's nothing else to do here but study. I really want to stay in school, but I don't seem to be able to get any work done. There are too many other important things to do around here.

1. _____

   _____

2. _____

   _____

Go to the next page.

Some possible responses:

1. Staying in school seems to be just as important as doing some of the extracurricular activities. I wonder which is more important of the two?

2. It sounds like you know what is needed to achieve your goal, yet you cannot bring yourself to work toward it. How can you remedy this situation?

    Both counselor responses point out the discrepancies that Joe has stated. Good confronting questions allow the client to examine the discrepancies—whether apparent or subtle—that are related to the main concern. This is the first step toward self-understanding and the ultimate resolution of problems.

Go to the next page.

SUMMARY

1. The objective of the counselor responses during Phase 2 is to help the client better understand him- or herself and the difficulties being experienced.
2. There are six types of questions that are helpful during Phase 2.
    a. Questions that obtain factual information
    b. Questions that provide specific examples of generalization
    c. Questions that clarify unclear terms
    d. Questions that focus the client
    e. Questions that redirect the client
    f. Questions that confront the client with discrepancies
3. Questions in Phase 2 should be open questions.
4. Questions described in Phase 2 can be threatening to the client and should be used only after the counselor/client relationship is well established.

EVALUATION

Evaluation is essential to the effective use of questions during the integration phase of the counseling process.

Once again, you must ask yourself the question: was the purpose of each question achieved? By examining what the client said, how it was said, and the verbal and nonverbal client behaviors, you can begin to determine if your questions were effective in bringing about the basic objectives of this counseling phase.

Ask yourself the following evaluation questions as the interview is proceeding and again after it has finished. If the answer is "yes" to most of these questions, then your use of questions for this phase is appropriate. If the answer is "no," then there is a strong likelihood that the basic objectives of Phase 2 are not being achieved.

It should be noted that, by the time you reach this phase of the counseling process, you should already be beginning to monitor your use of questions and evaluating their use or potential effectiveness even before you ask them.

QUESTIONING RESPONSE CHECKLIST: PHASE 2

1. Was there a purpose for each of the questions?
   yes   no   n/a

2. Did the answers provided by the client help to clarify and provide new meaning to issues discussed earlier?
   yes   no   n/a

3. Did I use focusing questions to help arrive at deeper levels of meaning to what was said?
yes   no   n/a

4. When the client began diverging from focus of the dialogue, did I use refocusing questions to return to the issues at hand?
yes   no   n/a

5. Was I able to recognize obvious and subtle inconsistencies between thoughts, feelings, and behaviors?
yes   no   n/a

6. Did I use confronting questions to point out inconsistencies?
yes   no   n/a

7. Could questions used have been better worked as reflections, clarifications, or direct statements?
yes   no   n/a

8. When the client used general or vague statements, did I use questions to bring about a more specific, concrete understanding of what was said?
yes   no   n/a

9. Were unclear terms used by the client clarified by my use of questions?
yes   no   n/a

10. Was I better able to understand and help the client to identify the elements of the concern in such a way as to promote future action or problem resolution?
yes   no   n/a

If you are able to positively evaluate your use of questions in Phase 2, then the essential elements for Phase 3 are present. It should be increasingly easier to monitor your use of questions. Further, you should be feeling more and more comfortable with your use of questioning as a counseling tool.

In the next chapter we'll be discussing Phase 3 of the counseling process. In this phase your evaluation will have considerable importance for the overall evaluation of your therapeutic efforts—that is, helping the client to achieve the ultimate counseling goal: resolution of the problem.

6

Phase 3: Action

Phases 1 and 2 of the counseling process facilitate client exploration and integration. During these first two phases the client/counselor relationship is established, the client's problem is explored and defined, and the client integrates an understanding of his or her experiences of self and the surrounding world. Phases 1 and 2 are valuable in and of themselves and often constitute the complete counseling process. In addition to facilitating exploration and integration, Phases 1 and 2 also prepare the client for Phase 3: action.

Phase 3 of the counseling process focuses directly on the client's behavior. The goal of Phase 3 is to help the client live more effectively. This is done by helping the client select a goal, outlining alternative action programs for goal attainment, evaluating programs outlined, selecting a program of action, and assessing the program after it is outlined. The message to the client in this stage of counseling is, "I have listened and understood what you have tried to express. Now let's focus on a goal and a plan of action that can help resolve the problem."

Phase 3 is appropriate only when the client has presented a problem to the counselor. (When no specific problem is presented or when the problem presented has no solution, Phase 3 is not helpful.) The client needs to express him- or herself fully, knowing that the counselor is listening with both understanding and respect. If a clear, definitive problem is eventually disclosed, then the process can advance to Phase 3. Moving to Phase 3 without a prior exploration and understanding of the problem will prove counterproductive. No matter how seemingly obvious and uncomplex the problem, it must be explored in depth before considering solutions. Considering solutions prematurely will likely lead to failure, since important aspects of the problem have not yet been thoroughly explored. Prior understanding of the problem increases the likelihood of its successful resolution.

In order to facilitate this process, the counselor uses solution-oriented responses to form manageable goals, and to suggest, evaluate, and select a plan of action and an assessment of behavior.

Questions readily serve as solution-oriented responses. They place more responsibility on the client and prompt him or her to work through the problem-solving process whenever possible with limited counselor assistance.

Questions are not the only solution-oriented response, but they are the most frequently and easily used. Before we discuss the various types of solution-oriented questions, a distinction must be made between solution-oriented responses and advice giving.

Solution-oriented responses help the client consider various possible solutions instead of insisting the client behave in a particular way. They take the form of a suggestion rather than a command and focus on the client's actions. Consider the following *inappropriate* counselor responses to this client statement:

Ronnie: I want to leave here and get back to work. I'm sick of it here. I can't wait to get out of the hospital but the doctor says I need more tests.

Ms. Howard: A. You must not leave yet.
   B. If I were you, I'd stay here and get the test before going back to work.
   C. There comes a time when most people don't like the hospital very much either, but they stick it out and you should, too.

Response A is an example of advice giving. It tells the client what to do. This response shows a lack of respect for the client as a person who can make decisions about what to do. Solution-oriented responses should indicate that the counselor thinks the client is capable of deciding what should be done.

In response B, the counselor tells the client what she would do if she were in his place. Being the person she is, she would not leave the hospital. However, it is Ronnie who has the problem and it is he who must decide what is best for him to do.

In response C, Ms. Howard tells Ronnie that others feel the same way about the hospital, and he should do what they did. This ignores the fact that Ronnie is a unique individual with his own perceptions, needs, and goals. How others respond may not be right for him.

Although all of the above responses appear to focus on what the client should do, none of them is very helpful. Good solution-oriented responses help clients work through the problem-solving process and help them decide what they want to do. They focus on the client and on individual responses to the problem.

Solution-oriented responses are usually of five types: (1) those that ask the client to select a manageable goal for the problem, (2) those that help the client consider various specific solutions, (3) those that help the client evaluate each solution, (4) those that help the client select a plan of action, and (5) those that help the client assess his or her own behavior.

SELECTING A GOAL

After the client has fully explored and defined the problem, it is time to move from problem integration to solution orientation. The solution-orientation stage of helping attempts to have the client set workable goals and means of achieving those goals. The counselor should shift to this third stage of helping when the client appears to have fully expressed him- or herself and the problem involved.

The shift to solution orientation might occur as quickly as ten minutes after the problem was first expressed, as delayed as two or three hours after the initial expression of the problem, or it may never occur. Many problems presented by clients never reach the solution-oriented stage of helping since they have no solution. The client who expresses them is not seeking answers but wants the satisfaction of being heard and understood.

It is important to stress that a shift to this stage of helping should only occur after the client has fully explored the problem. The shift in focus should occur when there is a repetition of thoughts and feelings being expressed by the client. If you attempt to shift from problem definition to solution orientation and the client either ignores your response or immediately attempts to redefine the problem, then your efforts are premature. Follow the client's lead and continue to explore and define the problem. Shift to the solution-finding process at a later time.

The first type of solution-orientation response is goal setting. This type of response is used to shift the client's focus from problem definition and exploration to solution orientation. More specifically, this type of response helps the client redefine one problem in terms of a workable goal. Goal-setting responses ask the client to think about what the situation might be like.

At the end of this phase of the solution-orientation process, the client should have defined a workable goal. A workable goal is one that is attainable and measurable and that can be readily defined. It should also be acceptable to the client's value system and his or her life direction. The counselor should help the client evaluate and select the best possible goal.

Example 1

Craig: Well, I don't know what else to say. I don't like living with my sister and her husband.

Ms. Reynolds: How would you like the situation to be?

Craig: I'd like to have a place of my own. I just don't know if I can afford it.

Example 2

Jenny: I guess I don't know what to do about the whole thing—my getting depressed and all.

Mr. Fenton: Instead of being depressed all the time, how would you like to feel?

Jenny: Happy, of course.

In the first example, the client has identified a specific problem. It may have taken him several hours to realize that living with his sister is a primary concern, but once that has been established a workable goal can be defined. The counselor will then suggest means of attaining that goal.

In the second example, the problem is still not clearly defined. The counselor's urging for a solution is premature, and Jenny's response is vague. The goal Jenny suggested, "being happy," is too general and not easily measurable. Perhaps later on in the counseling process a specific, more readily attainable goal could be suggested.

Read the following client statement and counselor questions. Which question asks the client to shift his focus from problem definition to goal selection?

Pablo: I guess at the bottom of everything is the fact that my wife makes more money than I do and that undermines my confidence.

Mrs. Rice: A. Would you like your wife to make less than you?
B. What would you like things to be like?
C. What are you going to do about it?

If you chose A, turn to page 152.
If you chose B, turn to page 153.
If you chose C, turn to page 154.

You chose A

Would you like your wife to make less than you?

You were to pick a question that asked the client to define a workable goal. This question suggests a workable goal and asks him to confirm or discount this goal. It is better for him to suggest a goal and then have the counselor help redefine it into workable terms.

Notice that the goal suggested by Mrs. Rice is clearly defined and easily measurable. However, it is phrased in terms of Pablo's wife's behavior rather than Pablo's behavior.

If you chose A, turn back one page and try again.

You chose B

What would you like things to be like?

This is the correct response. It asks the client to select a personal goal. Notice that the counselor uses the word *you* to emphasize Pablo's involvement in goal selection and the importance of his desires.

Did you notice that in response A, the counselor suggested a goal, and that in response C the counselor asks him to select a plan of action?

Turn to page 155.

You chose C

What are you going to do about it?

You were to choose a question that asked the client to define a workable goal. This is not it. This question asks him to suggest a plan of action. It assumes he already has a goal and wants to know how he is going to get there.

This response is helpful later on in the solution-oriented process but is premature at this point.

Turn back to page 151 and try again.

OUTLINING OPTIONS

After the client's problem has been explored and defined and a workable goal established, it is time to outline possible methods of goal attainment. The counselor should first encourage the client to suggest possible alternatives. The counselor should listen to the client's suggestions with interest and reinforce the client's efforts. Only after client suggestions are exhausted should the counselor make suggestions. But even now the counselor should be interested in client suggestions and input.

Questions are a means of soliciting suggestions from the client. They should ask the client, "What can *you* do about this type of problem?" Questions of this style put the responsibility on the client to solve his or her own problem instead of giving the counselor the responsibility of solving it. An open-ended question that seeks client suggestions demonstrates respect for the client as an independent person with the ability to solve problems. This goes along with the entire counseling process which should encourage the client to solve his or her own problem creatively.

Alternatives suggested by the client should not be evaluated immediately, since criticism might discourage a free flow of ideas. Instead, the counselor should encourage the client to verbalize all possible alternatives, since unworkable ideas may stimulate useful suggestions.

After client suggestions are exhausted, the counselor suggests alternatives for consideration by the client. This should happen only after the client's list of suggestions appears to be exhausted. When you are in the second phase of the solution process, your suggestions might facilitate further ideas for possible solutions from the client. Client modification of counselor suggestions should also be encouraged, since many times building ideas produces the best solution of all. Yet the client knows best what's right for him- or herself, and therefore should have primary responsibility for suggesting solutions.

One of the basic tasks of the solution-seeking process is when the counselor solicits possible solutions from the client. Which of the following is an example of a question that asks the client to suggest alternatives?

Gina: As I said, I don't know what to do about counseling. I don't want to stop coming, but it doesn't seem to be doing any good.

Mr. Green: A. Come with me and we will discuss this with another counselor.

B. Do you want to work with a different therapist tomorrow?

C. Do you have any ideas about what you might do about this situation?

If you chose A, turn to page 158.
If you chose B, turn to page 159.
If you chose C, turn to page 160.

You chose A

Come with me and we will discuss this with another counselor.

This is not an example of soliciting suggestions from the client, but rather of the counselor telling the client what he considers to be appropriate behavior. This response is in the form of a command rather than a question and is not a helpful solution-oriented response.

This response would be better if it were rephrased as, "Do you think it would help if we would discuss this with another counselor?" Notice that, rephrased, this response becomes a question, not a command. But even this is premature. It is important to first help the client express all her ideas and suggestions related to the problem and then have the counselor suggest his own ideas.

Turn back to page 157 and try again.

You chose B

Do you want to work with a different therapist tomorrow?

This is not the correct response. It is a solution-oriented response and is phrased as a suggestion, which is good, but offers a specific solution rather than helping the client suggest specific solutions. The second part of the action phase of helping is to facilitate the suggestion of solutions by the client. Only after the client has exhausted her own supply of possible solutions should the counselor make suggestions.

Turn back to page 157 and try again.

You chose C

> *Do you have any ideas about what you might do about this situation?*

This is the correct response. It is a solution-oriented response that helps the client explore the possible solutions to situations she has defined. This type of response accomplishes two things. First, it shifts the focus from goal setting to problem solving; second, it seeks specific suggestions from the client and therefore provides her with responsibility for her growth. Remember, this type of response is given only after the problem has already been fully explored and defined with the client and a workable goal established. This might be 15 minutes or several hours after the problem was initially introduced.

Advance to page 161.

To make sure that you've got it, select from the following questions the one that best seeks client suggestions.

Adrienne: My father is changing jobs and wants us to move right away. This is my last year of high school and I don't want to leave all my friends.

Ms. Meyers: A. Where are you moving?

B. Is there anything that could be done about it?

C. What suggestions do you have to cope with the problem?

If you chose A, go to page 162.
If you chose B, go to page 163.
If you chose C, go to page 164.

You chose A

Where are you moving?

This is not a question that helps the client focus on possible solutions to the problem. This is a questioning response that asks for more information. The counselor is trying to get more information from the client, probably so that she can suggest a more plausible solution. This is the type of response likely from beginning counselors. It is a signal that the earlier stages of helping were not given enough attention and that the counselor does not respect the client and her understanding of the problem.

Turn back to page 161 and try again.

You chose B

Is there anything that could be done about it?

This is a question that focuses on the consideration of possible solutions. However, this is a closed question which is intended to solicit a "yes" or "no" answer. The client will more likely respond "no," since the question implies a possible lack of solutions. If the client's response is "yes," the counselor queries her about it. This will then prompt the client to suggest solutions that she thought of herself or that may have been proposed to her by others.

Turn back to page 161 and try again.

You chose C

What suggestions do you have to cope with the problem?

This is the correct response. It will help the client suggest solutions to the problem. It places the responsibility for this phase of the problem solving on the client. It communicates to the client that the counselor respects her as a person and sees her as having the ability to work effectively on her own problems.

Advance to page 165.

Encouraging the client to suggest alternatives will provide a limited number of possible solutions for consideration. When the client appears to be without further suggestions, ask questions to encourage him or her further. Only when the client's repertoire of alternatives is completely exhausted should the counselor suggest possible alternatives. This will happen after the client has suggested one or several alternatives, but will be marked by a statement like, "I can't think of anything else," or "There are no other possibilities."

At this point, the counselor should offer suggestions for alternatives to those presented by the client. Counselor suggestions should be considered alternative solutions—not advice to be followed. In order to facilitate this, counselor alternatives should be in the form of questions.

If the client responds with statements that acknowledge counselor suggestons but dispute their value, you have probably progressed too fast through problem exploration and definition. Client responses that are clues to this are usually of the form, "Yes, but. . ." or "Yes, I hear your solution, but it is not a workable one for me."

However, if you have thoroughly worked through the earlier stages of helping, suggesting appropriate and relevant alternatives is easy. Helpful suggestions communicate a deep understanding of the client and further facilitate the developing relationship between the counselor and client.

After each counselor suggestion, the counselor should solicit alternatives from the client. This will encourage the client to build on the alternatives presented by the counselor and to suggest new alternatives stimulated by previous ideas. This process of mutual suggestions and problem solving is a very healthy one; remember, however, that the major responsibility for problem solving is with the client.

The phase of the solution-seeking process is completed when neither the counselor nor the client can think of further solutions. It is then time to move on to Phase 3 of the solution-seeking process—evaluating the alternatives.

In which of the following responses does the counselor suggest an alternative solution for the client to consider?

Harold: I kind of would like to ask my doctor when I can stop taking tranquilizers, but I'm afraid to ask him. He always acts so busy.

Mr. Wilconson: A. Don't be so shy. Next time you see him, ask him.
B. Why are you afraid to ask him?
C. Have you thought about asking your wife to call him at his office and talk to him?

If you chose A, go to page 168.
If you chose B, go to page 169.
If you chose C, go to page 170.

You chose A

Don't be so shy. Next time you see him, ask him.

This isn't the correct response. It is an example of advice giving—telling the client what to do—and is not a helpful response. The client has said he would like to ask his doctor when he can stop taking tranquilizers, but he's afraid to. Commanding him to do so probably won't make him any more able to do it. Further, the statement "Don't be so shy" communicates a lack of understanding and respect for him and his communication of fear and apprehension.

You were to select a response that presented an alternative for Harold. It should be phrased in the form of a suggestion for the client's consideration, not as a command. The counselor should offer solutions for the client to consider, and evaluate rather than presume his solution is appropriate.

Turn back to page 167 and try again.

You chose B

> *Why are you afraid to ask him?*

This is not the correct response. This is a questioning response asking for more information rather than a response that helps the client consider a specific solution to his problem. This is a "why" question, which is *never* appropriate. "Why" questions create defensiveness and seek justification from the client, assume authority, and serve no facilitative purpose.

The purpose of solution-oriented responses is not to evaluate client behavior, but rather to help the client when appropriate and to consider and evaluate possible solutions to his problems. You were to choose a solution-oriented response that suggested possible solutions for the client to consider. It would present a new idea to the client in the form of a question.

Turn back to page 167 and try again.

You chose C

> *Have you thought about asking your wife to call him at his office and talk to him?*

This is the correct response. It suggests a specific solution for the client to consider. Notice that it presents a new idea to the client in the form of a question. This response is only one of numerous solutions that could have been suggested by the counselor. Be sure to remember that specific counselor suggestions should only be made after the client has exhausted his ability to make suggestions.

Advance to page 171.

Since practice makes perfect, consider the following client statement and select the counselor response that is an example of a solution-oriented response and asks the client to consider a specific solution.

Barbara: Someone smashed in the side of my car when it was parked at the grocery store yesterday. It's over $1000 damage and we don't have insurance.

Mr. Warren: A. Have you considered trying to get insurance?

B. Have you considered talking to a bank regarding a short-term loan?

C. Do you have any ideas about how you will pay for the damages?

If you chose A, go to page 172.
If you chose B, go to page 173.
If you chose C, go to page 174.

You chose A

Have you considered trying to get insurance?

This is not the correct response. This response asks the client to consider a specific solution, but the solution suggested is not relevant to the problem presented. Barbara is concerned about finding $1000 to have her car repaired. Insurance will not help her with the problem, although it may help her avoid this problem in the future.

The correct response should suggest a specific solution relevant to the problem presented.

Turn back one page and try again.

You chose B

> *Have you considered talking to a bank regarding a short-term loan?*

This is the correct response. It suggests a solution relevant to the problem presented and serves two functions: it provides the client with an alternative to consider and it tells her about a service she might not know about. Notice that the new information is presented to the client in the form of a question. The counselor does not automatically assume that this is the best or most helpful solution possible.

Turn to page 175.

You chose C

Do you have any ideas about how you will pay for the damages?

This is not the correct response. It is a solution-oriented response that helps the client shift the focus from exploration and definition of the problem to suggesting specific alternatives. This is a helpful response, but it is not the correct response. The correct response should suggest a specific solution for the client to consider that is relevant to her problem.

Turn back to page 171 and try again.

EVALUATING THE ALTERNATIVES

We have already seen solution-oriented responses that help select goals and choose options. The third type of solution-oriented response focuses on the evaluation of alternatives.

The process of evaluation should begin only after all possible alternatives have been suggested. It's important not to overlap the phases of alternative suggestion and alternative evaluation, since if the alternatives are evaluated as they are initially presented it will discourage the suggestion of other alternatives.

This type of response asks the client, "What are the advantages and disadvantages of this particular solution?" or "What do you think would happen if you tried this solution?" It helps the client evaluate all the alternatives presented earlier in the problem-solving process. Discussing all the alternatives will increase the likelihood of the client selecting the most appropriate plan in the final phase of the problem-solving process.

While engaged in the process of evaluating solutions, the client will also think of new solutions. Since the best alternative is often arrived at from modification of previously stated alternatives, modification and additional suggestions should be encouraged.

This third phase of the problem-solving process is completed only after every possible solution has been independently evaluated. The pros and cons of each possible solution should be weighed and discussed. The evaluating process is shared by the counselor and the client, but most of the evaluating should be done by the client since he or she best understands the criteria for a successful solution.

Which of the following responses is an example of a solution-oriented response that helps the client evaluate a solution?

Beth: I don't want to get a divorce—not now anyhow. I can't manage without Jim.

Roger: A. If you don't get a divorce, what else can you do?
B. Maybe you should explore what would happen if you and your husband filed for a temporary separation.
C. How about moving in with your family for a while?

If you chose A, go to page 178.
If you chose B, go to page 179.
If you chose C, go to page 180.

You chose A

If you don't get a divorce, what else can you do?

This is not the correct response. It is a solution-oriented response but asks the client to suggest other possible alternatives rather than to evaluate a solution. It says to Beth, "What else can you do?" The correct response is intended to help the client consider her options and to evaluate the advantages and disadvantages of each.

Turn back to page 177 and choose the correct response.

You chose B

Maybe you should explore what would happen if you and your husband filed for a temporary separation.

This is the correct response. It is an example of a solution-oriented response that helps the client evaluate the consequences of a particular solution. This response asks Beth to do just that. The consequences of all the previously presented solutions should be considered before moving on to Phase 4 of the problem-solving process.

Turn to page 181.

You chose C

How about moving in with your family for a while?

This is a solution-oriented response, but it is not the correct type. You were asked to pick a response that focuses on evaluating a solution. This response asks Beth to consider a specific solution. The counselor is not asking the client what would happen if she moved in with her family, but merely to consider it as a possibility.

Turn back to page 177 and try again.

To give you more practice in recognizing the third type of solution-oriented response, read this client statement and select the counselor response that is a solution-oriented response and helps the client to evaluate a solution.

Jackie: My daughter has to be hospitalized for a long time. I have to choose between Good Hope and Three Sisters Hospitals. I don't know what to do.

Ms. Tucker: A. You should send her to Good Hope. They have a better reputation.

B. How do you think things would work out if you chose Three Sisters?

C. Could you visit both Good Hope and Three Sisters and see how you like them?

If you chose A, go to page 182.
If you chose B, go to page 183.
If you chose C, go to page 184.

You chose A

You should send her to Good Hope. They have a better reputation.

This is not a solution-oriented response that helps the client evaluate a solution. In this response the counselor presents the client with her personal evaluation of the two hospitals. The statement, "You should send her to Good Hope. They have a better reputation" really says, "I think you should go to Good Hope. I hear they have a better reputation." Counselors should encourage clients to explore the possibilities involved but should refrain from providing personal opinions. Statements that tell the client what to do are never helpful during any phase of the problem-solving process.

Turn back one page and try again.

You chose B

How do you think things would work out if you chose Three Sisters?

This is the correct response. It is an example of a solution-oriented response that helps the client evaluate a specific solution. The "solution" is choosing Three Sisters Hospital. The counselor statement, phrased as a question, suggests that the client consider the possible consequences of making this choice.

The next step would be to consider the consequences of choosing Good Hope Hospital, in addition to other solutions suggested. The consequences of each of these should be considered in detail; then the client can choose one of these solutions.

Turn to page 185.

You chose C

Could you visit both Good Hope and Three Sisters and see how you like them?

This is a solution-oriented response, but it is not the type you were asked to choose. You were asked to select a solution-oriented response that would help the client consider the consequences of selecting a particular solution. This response helps the client to focus on a specific solution. Notice that the specific solution is suggested by the counselor and not presented as a solution the client must accept. The solution suggested is a valuable one, since it will eventually help the client select a plan of action based on knowledge she obtained herself.

Turn back to page 181 and try again.

SELECTING A PLAN OF ACTION

Selecting a plan of action is the next to last phase of the problem-solving process. The purpose of this phase is to help the client decide what she or he wants to do about the problem. It communicates the necessity of taking action. It suggests that discussing the problem isn't enough; a change in behavior should follow. Responses in this phase of the process ask the client, "What do you want to do about your problem?" The decision and responsibility for action both rest with the client since it is the client alone who will experience the consequences of the behavior.

This phase of the helping process should flow easily from the previous stages of helping, assuming they were fully developed. Failure to attend fully to any of the previous stages of helping will make decision-making impossible or difficult for the client. Of course, the client should not be encouraged to make a decision until all suggested alternatives have been evaluated.

This phase of the problem-solving process is intended to begin to bring some closure to the client's consideration of a specific problem, but it may or may not mean the end of the counseling process. The client may want to keep evaluating the solutions or consider other problems.

Read the client statement and pick the counselor response that helps the client select a plan of action.

Rudolph: My parents are getting a divorce and I have to choose which one I want to live with. I don't know what to do.

Diana: A. You should stay with your mother. She's going to need a man around the house to help her.

B. How do you think it would work out if you moved in with your father?

C. We've outlined just about all your options; what do you think you'd like to do?

If you chose A, go to page 188.
If you chose B, go to page 189.
If you chose C, go to page 190.

You chose A

> *You should stay with your mother. She's going to need a man around the house to help her.*

This is not a solution-oriented response that helps the client select a plan of action. This response is an example of advice giving. The counselor is selecting a plan of action for the client that is contrary to the entire problem-solving process. The objective of the problem-solving process is for the client to suggest, evaluate, and select a plan of action, since it is he who has the problem and best understands it.

You were to choose the response that asked the client to select a plan of action. The correct response will be in the form of a question and place the major responsibility for problem solving on the client.

Turn back one page and try again.

You chose B

How do you think it would work out if you moved in with your father?

This is not a solution-oriented response that helps the client select a plan of action. Instead, this response helps the client evaluate a particular specific solution. The counselor's statement suggests that Rudolph consider the advantages and disadvantages of living with his father.

The correct response would ask Rudolph to make a decision regarding whom he wants to live with. It should be phrased in the form of a question and place the responsibility for the decision with him.

Turn back to page 187 and try again.

You chose C

We've outlined just about all your options; what do you think you'd like to do?

This is the correct response. It asks the client to select a plan of action. Notice that the responsibility for the selection of an alternative and for action rests with the client, since he will deal with the consequences of his behavior.

Proceed to the next page.

Read the client statement and select the counselor response that helps the client select a plan of action.

Marcel: I don't want my boss to see me like this. I'm afraid of losing my job. When I've been doing drugs, I'm no good at work at all.

Andy: A. Don't let it get you down. If you have a good work record, you can afford to lose a day.

B. You are supposed to be at work in an hour. What do you want to do?

C. Do you have any ideas what you might do?

If you chose A, go to page 192.

If you chose B, go to page 193.

If you chose C, go to page 194.

You chose A

Don't let it get you down. If you have a good work record, you can afford to lose a day.

This is not the correct response. This response does not ask the client to select a plan of action, nor does it facilitate the problem-solving process. The response communicates a lack of understanding and respect to the client. It says, "I don't appreciate your concern and fears."

It further assumes information about the client's work record and employment status that is unknown to the counselor. The client might lose his job after a day's absence.

The correct response asks the client to select a plan of action. It says, "What do you want to do?"

Turn back one page and try again.

You chose B

You're supposed to be at work in an hour. What do you want to do?

This is the correct response. It asks the client to make a decision. It tells Marcel to see the problem and time constraints realistically and to make a decision.

Turn to page 195.

You chose C

Do you have any ideas what you might do?

This is not the correct response. It is a solution-oriented response and asks the client what he *might* do. It shifts the focus to problem exploration but it does not ask the client to make a decision. The correct response asks the client to make a decision based on an integration of his understanding of the problem, his alternatives, and their consequences.

Turn back to page 191 and choose the correct response.

ASSESSING CLIENT ACTION

Assessing client action is the process in which both the counselor and client evaluate the effectiveness of a decision made by the client during the problem-solving process. The evaluation takes place after the client has attempted the solution decided on. Evaluating client action is the final step in the problem-solving process, but it is also the most critical step in the process. It provides the client with the necessary connection between the counseling process and the client's behavior outside the counseling environment. It also provides the client with a connection between one counseling session and another, and gives the client a means for evaluating the counseling process. Finally, inquiring about the client's success or failure at attempting the solutions considered communicates to the client the counselor's real concern.

After the client has selected a goal, listed alternative methods of attaining that goal, evaluated the alternatives, and selected from among them, it is time for the client to act on the selection. The client should try to change his or her behavior outside the counseling setting in the direction decided on during the problem-solving process. If the client does not want to try to change behavior in this way, the alternative selected should be re-evaluated and another selection made. If the client does not want to change his or her behavior at all, the purpose and usefulness of counseling should be discussed.

When the client does wish to change behavior in the direction selected during the problem-solving process, the process then proceeds. The client should now be given time to test out and observe the effect of his or her selection in the real world. The time necessary for this test can be anywhere from one day to several months, depending on the solution selected. For example, a male client who decided his relationship with his mother might be aided by more truthfulness on his part might decide to discuss his past dishonesty with his mother. The short-term effects of his decision can be evaluated immediately after his discussion with his mother.

On the other hand, if a client decides she can get a better job after she goes to school, she has to wait several months or years to evaluate the effect of her decision. First, she has to apply to school and then wait for the next term to start. After she begins to attend classes, she can evaluate her initial reaction, but only after she has completed her program and obtained a new job can she evaluate the total effectiveness of her decision. This process of going to school to get a better job might take several years and continue past the end of the counseling relationship. Thus, the time delay between selection and evaluation of an alternative may vary, but whenever possible the counselor should help the client evaluate the effectiveness of the decision during the counseling process.

The process of assessing client action is a fairly straightforward one. It employs several of the skills discussed earlier in this text. First, the counselor should be concerned with the client's experience, as well as his or her cognitive and affective reaction to that experience. Second, the client should be primarily responsible for the evaluation since it is his or her experience. Third, the counselor should employ open questions to facilitate the evaluation process.

Consider the previously mentioned example of the client who wanted to have a more honest relationship with his mother. The client had decided to tell his mother that he has not been spending his evenings studying at the library but rather with his girlfriend. The counselor might facilitate consideration of the results of such a discussion in the following way:

Mr. Maloney: Last week you decided you wanted to talk to your mother about your spending time with your girlfriend. What did you do about this idea?

Shawn: I talked to her.

Mr. Maloney: Can you tell me about the conversation?

Shawn: Sure. Last week after I left here. . . .

Notice that the counselor first asked whether or not Shawn tried to discuss the matter with his mother. Since he said he did, a discussion of the interaction and its consequences should follow. It is not only important to examine what happened and what the client thought and felt about it, but also to see if the desired results were attained: that is, can the client now honestly spend time with his girlfriend?

If Shawn had not discussed the issue with his mother, consideration of the causes would have been appropriate. Failure to act is usually an indication that the previous stages of helping were not fully explored and subsequently the correct solution was not reached. That knowledge is also helpful to the client.

Martha is a woman of 35 with two small children. Her husband works long hours while she spends all day with the children. She'd like to get a job because she wants to get out more and because they need the money, yet she feels guilty about leaving her chidren with a babysitter. After several weeks of counseling, Martha decided to enroll her children in nursery school and look for a part-time job. Last week the counselor suggested that she spend this week trying to find a suitable nursery school so that her guilt feelings about leaving the children would be eliminated.

Read the following items and select the counselor question that best begins the assessment process.

Mr. Russo: A. Did you look at any nursery schools this week?
B. How did you feel about the nursery schools you looked at?
C. Last week we discussed your finding a nursery school for the children. What did you do to move toward this goal?

If you chose A, turn to page 198.
If you chose B, turn to page 199.
If you chose C, turn to page 200.

You chose A

Did you look at any nursery schools this week?

This is not the best response. It is a closed question and will solicit a "yes" or "no" response from the client. A better response would help her freely discuss her behavior during this past week as it relates to the problem under consideration.

Turn back one page and try again.

You chose B

How do you feel about the nursery schools you looked at?

This is not the most helpful response. This question assumes that Martha did examine nursery schools this past week, which may or may not be true. This question also asks her to reveal her feelings about the schools before obtaining her cognitive reaction to them. This response might prove helpful later on. However, right now a better response would help her freely discuss her behavior this past week as it relates to the problem being considered.

Turn back to page 197 and try again.

You chose C

> *Last week we discussed your finding a nursery school for the children. What did you do to move toward this goal?*

This is the correct response. It gives the client the freedom to discuss what she has done this past week. Did you notice that response A was a closed question? Response B assumed the client had examined nursery schools and was prematurely requesting the disclosure of client feelings.

Proceed to the next page.

SUMMARY

1. Solution-oriented responses should help the client engage in the problem-solving process and select a satisfactory solution.
2. There are six types of solution-oriented responses:
   a. Responses that help the client shift from exploration of the problem to establishment of a reasonable goal.
   b. Responses that help the client outline possible solutions.
   c. Responses when the counselor suggests solutions.
   d. Responses that help the client evaluate specific solutions.
   e. Responses that help the client select a plan of action.
   f. Responses that help the client assess action taken.
3. Solution-oriented responses should be phrased as suggestions in question form, such as:
   a. "What would you like . . .?"
   b. "What do you think you can do about . . .?"
   c. "Have you considered . . .?"
   d. "What would happen if . . .?"
   e. "What are you going to do . . .?"
   f. "How did your plan work out . . .?"
4. Solution-oriented responses are not appropriate at the beginning of a conversation with a client who is presenting a problem. They should be used only after the problem situation has been thoroughly explored and defined.
5. Solution-oriented responses are usually in the form of questions.

EVALUATION

Evaluation is in many ways the most important phase of the process, because it is here that the ultimate goals of counseling will be achieved or not achieved. The counselor's efforts in Phase 3 may be the most difficult and frustrating of the three phases, because this is where the client must *do* something—must undertake some action or make some decision. It is in this phase that problem resolution occurs. For these reasons, continuous evaluation throughout is essential. Evaluation allows us to be aware of progress, to know when counseling can terminate, and to modify our efforts when they are not successful.

More importantly, this phase provides the external evaluation about whether our efforts toward action are having any impact on the client's goals for counseling—probably the most important aspect of any counseling evaluation.

The questions counselors ask themselves about the progress they are making will relate to two situations: what they are doing and saying in the actual counseling session, and what is happening to the client's behavior outside the counseling environment. Part of this evaluation is directed toward the types of questions posed in dialogues with the client and part is related to the overall objectives of the client in counseling.

If the evaluation is continuous and ongoing throughout this stage, counselors can make adjustments where needed. If it is not, their efforts will be reduced to trial and error interventions and will ultimately prove counterproductive to helping efforts. The following questions should help evaluate if the goals for the action phase of counseling are achieved and if the use of questions is contributing to this achievement.

As in Phases 1 and 2, the answers to these questions should be "yes." If not, the objectives of this phase are not being met and problem resolution will not occur.

QUESTIONING RESPONSE CHECKLIST: PHASE 3

1. Do both the client and I understand the problem and the situation that has been presented?
   yes   no   n/a

2. Have I used solution-oriented responses to help the client formulate manageable goals for counseling?
   yes   no   n/a

3. Were these goals mutually agreed upon?
   yes   no   n/a

4. Did the solution-oriented responses used help the client to work through the problem-solving process?
   yes   no   n/a

5. Did the solution-oriented responses avoid advice giving?
   yes   no   n/a

6. Did the solution-oriented responses help the client consider various specific solutions and alternatives?
   yes   no   n/a

7. Did my use of questions help the client to understand and explore the ramifications and consequences of the possible solutions and alternatives?
   yes   no   n/a

8. Did my use of questions and solution-oriented responses help the

client to realistically evaluate each solution?
yes   no   n/a

9. Did my solution-oriented responses help the client to select an appropriate course of action?
yes   no   n/a

10. Did my questions help to determine whether the course of action was effective?
yes   no   n/a

11. If the course of action was not effective, did my use of questions help to examine and evaluate the reasons for the ineffectiveness?
yes   no   n/a

12. Did my solution-oriented response help define new goals or formulate new alternative courses of action in response to previous ineffectiveness?
yes   no   n/a

13 Do I have an accurate conception of when to terminate with the client?
yes   no   n/a

14. Are the client and I in agreement about what constitutes successful goal achievement?
yes   no   n/a

15. Do I have some established procedure to follow up the client at a later time?
yes   no   n/a

16. Can I feel assured in believing that I have made my best effort with this client?
yes   no   n/a

17. If not, are there specific things I can improve for future clients?
yes   no   n/a

The following questions should also be answered as part of every post-counseling client evaluation:

1. What has the client learned from this experience?
2. What have I learned from this experience?
3. How can I apply what has been learned to future counseling efforts?

If you can ask yourself these questions, the answers should provide a rich source of evaluation information about the experience of counseling that has just concluded. Questions such as these must be asked at some point in Phase 3 of the counseling process if counselor growth and development is to occur. Unless we can learn from what we do—and do what we learn—we will never advance beyond elementary trial and error efforts, and both the client and counselor will suffer.

The next chapter will present transcripts of counseling sessions demonstrating the use of questions in the various phases of the process. This should help you gain additional perspectives on questions as they are actually used at various phases of the counseling process.

7

Questions: Examples in Actual Practice

In this chapter, we will present two excerpts from counseling sessions to illustrate the use of questions during the counseling process. The first transcript demonstrates how questions can be used in the initial counseling session—Phase 1; the second demonstrates the use of questions in Phase 2. Take special note of the comments to the right of the transcripts that explain the counselor's rationale and purpose throughout the dialogues.

After you have read the two transcripts, note the differences between the purposes of the two sessions, keeping in mind the discussion of the use of questions in the counseling process in Chapter 2. Be sure to note how the use of questions facilitates the counselor's overall objectives for the two phases of the counseling process.

TRANSCRIPT 1

The following is a transcript of an initial counseling session. Note how questions can be used to facilitate the extent and direction of the interview. The client, Sally, is a 19-year-old college sophomore experiencing difficulty in living with her roommate.

Counselor: Come in, Sally. How are you?

Sally: Fine.

Counselor: Make yourself comfortable. What is it we can do for you?

The first two counselor questions open the interview and help to set the client at ease.

Sally: Well, I'm having a real problem with my roommate and I really don't know what to do about it.

Counselor: Could you tell me a little about the situation?

This response is an open invitation to talk. It allows the client to express herself in her own way and to discuss what she feels is important.

Sally: Well, Jean, my roommate, and I have not been able to get along since school started. She seems so inconsiderate. Almost everything she does gets on my nerves. All we do is fight and argue about everything. I wish we didn't have to live together.

Counselor: It sounds like this situation is pretty upsetting.

The counselor is using a reflection of feeling to help the client explore some of her feelings about the situation.

Sally: You bet! I can't get any school work done. She always has her boy friends over, until all hours of the night. I really get angry and then I wind up leaving the room.

Counselor: Could you tell me a little bit about how you feel when you do leave your room?

The counselor is continuing in exploration of feelings, and this question is attempting to further explore the situation.

Sally: Well, it really bothers me that I have to leave or give in. I mean, why can't she go somewhere with her boyfriend? It's just as much my room as it is hers.

Counselor: Uh huh.

This response, small as it may seem, will help to get the client to pursue this line of discussion. It also helps convey that the counselor is attending to what the client is saying.

Sally: It really makes me mad the more I think about it.

Counselor: How do you mean?

This question will help clarify what the client means in her previous response.

Sally: Well, I feel mad at myself for not being able to do something about it.

Counselor: So, on one hand you feel upset because of what your roommate is doing, and on the other, you feel upset because of how you are reacting or are forced to react to the situation. Is that about right?

The counselor is summarizing and further clarifying the relationship between Sally's situation and her feelings about it. The question at the end is used to seek the client's corroboration.

Sally: Yes, that's exactly how I feel. I really need to do something about it.

Counselor: Could we back up for a second? Maybe you could tell me something more about the things that happen between you and Jean.

The counselor is trying to re-direct the client to the specific issues in her relationship with her roommate. Now that some indication of the problem is present, a more specific problem statement can be sought. This will aid the client and counselor when it comes time to formulate goals for the counseling.

Sally: Ok, well, it started almost from the time we first met. She just has no feelings for other people— well, at least not for me anyway. She does whatever she pleases. I try to be nice and think of her. I even try to talk

to her about it. But it
doesn't seem to work. She
just disregards my rights.

Counselor: Could you tell me
about that?

An open-ended question such as
this will allow the client to
expand on the issue of "talking
to her roommate." This issue
will obviously play a vital role
in the strategies used to
ultimately solve the problem.

Sally: Well, at first I just didn't
say anything. I kept it in.
It really made me feel like a
jerk. I was afraid to say anything because I didn't want
her to dislike me.

Counselor: Uh huh. (pause)

The pause of silence allows the
client to continue talking about
this new concern she has just
raised.

Sally: Well, nothing ever changed.
Then one day I was
studying and she came
in with her boyfriend and
they just sat on the bed
listening to the radio. I
got so mad, I just lost my
temper.

Counselor: It must be difficult
wanting someone to like
you and trying so hard and
then getting so upset by it.

This is a subtle response to
redirect the client's feelings
to her previous response. This
seems important to the resolution of Sally's problem.

Sally: Well, I've tried talking
to her several times, but
we just end up arguing.
Now I really feel bad whenever I have to go back to my
room after class.

Counselor: You've tried to talk
to her about the problems
but it hasn't seemed to
work, and now you really

The counselor is summarizing
the overall presenting problem.
This will help lead Sally into
goal setting and problem solving.

don't know what to do next.
Is that what you see as the
overall problem?

Sally: Yes, that's about right.

Counselor: Well, Sally, how
    would you like to see this
    situation resolved?

The counselor has helped the
client to define the problem
and explore the issues. Now
questioning is being used to
move toward the formulation of
a counseling goal.

Sally: Well, I guess I'd like
    to get a new roommate. But
    I don't suppose that's
    possible this early in the
    term. Sometimes I think
    that maybe I'm to blame,
    too. Maybe it would be the
    same with a new roommate
    or even worse!

Counselor: It sounds like you're
    feeling some responsibility
    for the situation, too.

The counselor is helping Sally
explore a new dimension to her
problem that she has introduced. This may be directly
relevant to the ultimate resolution of the roommate situation.

Sally: I really don't know.
    I guess there are things
    I could have done, too, but
    I was just too angry with
    her. Maybe I'd feel better
    if we could both get along
    and work this thing out. I
    really don't want to move
    out anyway.

Counselor: Uh huh. How do you
    think you can resolve
    this problem?

The counselor is using the
question to press Sally for a
commitment to set a counseling
goal to work toward.

Sally: Maybe you could help me
    figure out some way to
    work out our differences
    so we could live together—
    some kind of compromise.

Maybe I'm using the wrong approach when I try to talk to Jean. Maybe you could help me do something about that.

Counselor: I think that might be a good goal to work toward.

Sally: Well, it's worth a try. I've tried everything else.

Counselor: Okay. Well, let me summarize where we are then. It sounds like you want to work out some type of compromise with Jean. This would entail developing some effective ways to communicate with each other. So this is our goal for counseling. Does that sound correct?

The counselor is verifying the goal and plan of action that has been reached with Sally.

Sally: Yes. I don't think it's going to be easy, but I've got to work something out soon.

Counselor: Have you thought about what has happened in the past whenever you two talked about your differences?

After the goal has been stated and mutually agreed on, the counselor inquires about problem-solving strategies.

Sally: Well, no, I haven't. I've always just gotten so mad that I usually get up and leave or else she will. I usually try to forget what happens.

Counselor: How are things between you two after one of these incidents is forgotten?

The open-ended question is used to further exploration.

Sally: Very cool. We both are cordial to each other. But, boy, you can tell there's

something icy in the air.
You know what I mean?

Counselor: Well, I suspect that if you feel this way toward Jean, it's a good bet that she feels about the same toward you.

This response is a conclusion stated to help Sally see that it is not only her feelings that are involved, but her roommate's as well. The counselor wants the client to understand that the feelings of both will be involved if any compromise is to be reached.

Sally: I never thought of it that way.

Counselor: This may be a good approach to your problem. Maybe you could think about some of the things you do that irritate Jean and some of the things she does that irritate you. Write them down on paper if you wish. These can be the issues we discuss at our next visit. Does this sound like something you would like to start working on?

The counselor is ending with a suggested approach for Sally to do something for their next visit. The question at the end serves to confirm her commitment to her goal for counseling; the information will be helpful for a resolution to the problem.

TRANSCRIPT 2

The following is a transcript of a third session with an unmarried female client in her early thirties. Throughout the session, the counselor presses for specific, concrete examples. The counselor tries to help the client integrate separate occurrences and perceptions to help her understand that what she is experiencing is not a series of unrelated chance occurrences. The counselor focuses attention on immediate feelings and wraps up the session with a series of summarizing questions.

Linda: I feel like life is playing me a dirty trick. Without my doing anything, my life gets fouled up.

Counselor: Will you help me understand exactly what you mean by giving a specific example or two?

The counselor uses a question to invite the client to be more concrete. The client's initial statement is too vague to be readily understood.

Linda: Yeah, oh sure. I had just had my car overhauled when some drunk totaled it while it was parked in front of my house. The money I got from the insurance didn't even cover my repair bill, so now I'm driving a five-year-old junker just to get around . . . Then take this guy I'm hooked on. I didn't ask to meet him or fall in love with him. I was just beginning to get my act together when he began to put the rush on me. I mean he just happened to be in my class. He treated me like a queen for four months and I fell for him. Now he treats me like dirt. I know he's bad for me and screwed-up himself, but I can't stop loving him. I just keep wishing things would be like they were the first four months. I know they won't ever be like that again. So why did he have to get into my life in the first place? I don't want . . . I never wanted all the crap I'm getting now.

Counselor: Is it possible that these two examples don't fall in the same category? Is it possible that your car being hit was simply a random accident but that

The client has offered her examples as though they are identical. The counselor invites the client to share in the analysis of these to examples against a backdrop suggested by the you are very much involved in developing whatever relationship you have with this fellow?

counselor that these examples really are different. The "Is it possible . . .?" lead allows the client to disagree with the counselor without strongly confronting the counselor's perception. The types of questions the counselor uses here offer input but also offer the client freedom to disagree.

Linda: Yeah, oh sure . . . . Well, I was just giving you examples. You see I did not ask to get into either mess and if I had known their outcomes I would have done something to prevent them.

Even this gentle questioning approach seems to disturb the client. A counselor cannot know the degree of comfort or uneasiness in the client. The counselor has gambled with a response that might be more pointed than the client is ready to accept.

Counselor: You were trying to help me understand that there are undesirable aspects of your life which you would never have allowed, given some indication of how they would turn out.

The counselor is sensitive to the uneasiness his previous questions may have stimulated in the client, so he selects a very understanding and suportive reflective response to which the client strongly replies.

Linda: You bet your booties. If a guy came up to me and said he'd never have enough money to take me out, couldn't call me when he was going to be late, and didn't want me to make any demands on him but wanted to date me, I'd laugh in his face.

Counselor: I have a feeling that apart from giving specific examples your relationship with your boyfriend is a real and present concern.

The counselor tries an analytic hunch on the client, who seems to affirm it.

Linda: Well, wouldn't you be

concerned if you could
never count on your wife
coming home?

Counselor: Is your relationship
with your boyfriend the
thing you want to talk
about now or is there some
other topic you'd rather
pursue?

The counselor is now attempting
to ascertain if the client wants
to pursue the topic of the boyfriend. The counselor seems
right in wondering whether the
client is prepared to explore this
aspect of her life.

Linda: Well, you suggested that
I had something to do with
getting involved with him.
That's crap. I even stood
him up the first time he
asked me out. I didn't
ask him out. I didn't put
him in that class. He put
the rush on me. I didn't ask
for it. I was getting
squared away and had
begun dating a good-
looking fellow. This guy
is not good looking—even
though he turns me on.

Counselor: I have a hunch that
you'd like to talk about
your relationship with this
boy now but are hesitant to
take responsibility for
doing it. Do you indeed
want to spend time on this
topic now?

The counselor is challenging
the client to take responsibility
for her actions, at least for the
action of discussing this relationship. Exploration of this topic
at this time is up to the client.

Linda: Well, if you want to . . . .

Counselor: One of the concerns
in your life we can spend
time on is your relationship
with your boyfriend. There
are others as well, I'm
sure. Which do *you* want to
pursue?

Direct questions are used here
to communicate the challenge.

Linda: The boyfriend, I suppose.

Counselor: Okay. How would you like to begin?

Here the counselor uses an open invitation to begin.

Linda: Well . . . I met this guy in a class I was taking . . . and I noticed him right off. I mean, I saw him looking at me during class and somehow I knew he was going to ask me out. But he didn't for more than half the semester, even though we sort of met after class on the steps and things and said "Hi." I don't think he was shy or anything. I mean, I could feel him looking down my dress. But he never said, "How about a beer" or anything. Then one day in November he said "How about a beer after class?" I said I couldn't; I had another appointment. I really did have one. So he said, "How about tomorrow?" and I said, "Maybe." So he said he'd be at the campus tavern at 7:00 p.m. Could I come? I said maybe, but then didn't show up. I figured if he were serious he'd ask again, and if he was going to stand me up, I didn't want to be played the fool. Well, he showed up and I didn't. And he couldn't get in touch with me because he didn't have my phone number. I mean,

During this client narration, the counselor stores information and begins the analytic process. He can generate a variety of hunches that might lead to questions exploring one facet or another of the client's narration, such as asking her what caused her to think the boy might stand her up in the first place. The counselor's hunch might be that his client is quite unsure of her attractiveness and is protecting herself before being insulted. The counselor chooses not to interrupt. This fits with our approach of allowing themes to develop in the client's narration. Each time a client touches a continuing topic, even from a slightly different angle, the probability of the counselor's hunch about that topic being correct increases. By the end of this client narration, the counselor might have developed a strong hunch that Linda feels quite insecure. He might be right that her self-concept is low, but playing out such a hunch at this point in the relationship would be very risky.

it's in the phone book and
all, but he didn't know where
I lived. So the next class, I
was late and he caught
me afterward to ask
where I had been. I made
up some story and told
him I didn't have his
phone number so I
couldn't call him. Well, he
said he understood and
would I like to go to
dinner with him the next
day. I said, "Okay." So he
came by my apartment to
pick me up. We had a
wonderful time. We went
back to my place and
listened to music
afterward. We didn't even
kiss; just talked. He said
he was married but was
leaving his wife; that they
had never gotten along.
They had been married
eight years. Well, he got
my phone number and
the one at work, and
before I saw him the next
night he had called me
three times. I saw him
every day for the next
week. We didn't do
anything spectacular but
he was so attentive. I even
played hard to get. I
mean, I don't like when
men I don't love paw me.
But by the end of the
week we were in bed
together. It was terrific
and he started to come
over every night. I didn't
understand how he could
do it and stay late and

all—being married, you know—but he did. We even started to take showers together. I was in seventh heaven. I couldn't believe it was real. In about a month he left his wife and moved in with me. I know it sounds silly but it seemed so right then. We seemed to have so much in common and he was even talking about our having a farm or cabin in the woods together. I couldn't believe it was happening to me.

Counselor: It sounds as though some chemistry was working between the two of you from the very beginning. You checked it out for a while, but when the mix started, well, it was just wonderful.

Instead, the counselor uses a reflective response to let the client know he was hearing and to encourage more self-disclosure.

Linda: Was it! For four months everything was great. He was always home, predict-ably. If he wasn't, he'd call. We were making love every night, even most mornings. We went away on week-ends. He'd help with the housework since I was working and he wasn't . . . . Then things started to change. He got a job, which I thought was good. But he started coming home late some days. He said he had to work late, but it made me frantic. I asked him why he couldn't call to let me know he'd be late. He said

The picture of a client with great need for attention and affection develops in this response, along with other indications of feelings of insecurity: "All I could think of was that he was with another woman" and "I won't play second to any woman."

he was out on the truck.
He works for a nursery, and
there was no phone
available. Well, I said that
was crazy, there was always
a phone available if you are
in a truck. Well, he said he
couldn't call and I had no
right to know where he was
anyhow. I said where did
he get that crap. Here I was
practically married to him.
He's living in my place and
I'm holding dinner for him
and he doesn't show . . . .
It's just common courtesy
. . . . He said what he did
away from me was his
business and I should keep
my nose out of it. All I could
think of was that he was
with another woman. If he
were, I'd drop him like a
hot potato. I won't play
second to any woman. But
I couldn't prove anything
and he denied it. Well, even
if he did have to work late
he could at least call me . . . .
Then, well . . . one day he
was about an hour late so I
called his work. The guy on
the phone said Mac—that's
my boyfriend—left about
3:00 p.m. Well, that was two-
and-a-half hours earlier.
I heard a lot of laughing
in the background; then
the guy said, "Could I take
a message?" I said no and
hung up. Well, when Mac
got home about 8:00 p.m.,
I was wild. The food was
cold and I was frantic.
I mean, you should see how
I get. I guess he tried to

explain, but it was crap. I just yelled and he walked out . . . . There's no excuse for not calling . . . . He came back later, but things weren't the same . . . . He got his divorce during this time. We were still making love but things just didn't seem the same to me. He was less attentive and meaner. I confronted him about this several times but he denied that anything was different. Then on August 5, I came home to find his stuff gone. I got a call a little later from one of his friends to tell me Mac had moved out. The _____ didn't have the courage to call me himself. (The client begins to cry softly.)

Counselor: His moving out that way really hurt.

The counselor, instead of processing hunches here, picks up on the client's pain. The client has previously given evidence of some hesitancy in discussing the boyfriend topic; the counselor seems right in not making penetrating analytic statements or questions here. In other circumstances the counselor might choose to explore the client's awareness of her own feelings of insecurity, needs, and self-protective behavior, but here a gentle allowing of the client to contact her present feelings is better.

Linda: Uh huh. (Sob)

Counselor: Can you allow your-

This question is an invitation

self to get deeply in touch with your hurt?

to the client, but it also allows her to back away from the topic if the experience of separation is too painful.

Linda: (Nods affirmation)

Counselor: Where do you feel the hurt?

Having assured himself that the client feels able to get in touch with her hurt, the counselor uses a question to move the client into contact with her present feeling.

Linda: Mainly in my stomach.

Counselor: Describe it to me.

What appears here as a counselor command could just as easily have been put as an invitation: "Will you describe the pain?" The counselor is feeling somewhat stronger in interacting with the client and feels he can stimulate a clear reply with a more forceful lead.

Linda: I feel like I've been punched . . . doubled over . . . but I also want to throw up.

Counselor: You're even sitting that way. You appear to me to be protecting your stomach.

The counselor is entering more vigorously into the information sharing process.

Linda: I am, in a way. I don't want to be hit again.

Counselor: What about the feeling of wanting to throw up?

This question indicates that the counselor heard two messages: (1) feeling like having been punched, and (2) wanting to throw up. He assesses both messages as important. In the client's response immediately preceding this question only one message was mentioned, so the counselor seems wise to use a question to direct the client's attention to the second message.

Linda: Well, I feel like throwing up, just having it all come up in a big stream, but I can't.

Counselor: You feel like there is something you'd like to just vomit up, but can't.

This is a reflective response, as is the next, which is also a partial summary. The client corrects it in her reply. The counselor's caution in not rushing his client and in allowing her to feel she can disagree with him pays off.

Linda: Yes! I also have the vague feeling that I'd like for him to be there.

Counselor: Let's see . . . you feel like you've been punched in the gut and your body seems to be protectively wrapped around your stomach. You also feel like throwing up in Mac's presence.

Linda: Not in front of him—on him.

Counselor: Try to get even more deeply involved with this feeling.

The counselor's statement here could have been placed as the polite invitation: "Will you try . . .?"

Linda: I don't know . . . . I kind of see him standing there covered with it . . . but the thought goes away right away.

Counselor: Do you feel angry— even vindictive—when you have this thought?

Through the use of this question the counselor is testing out an hypothesis. Occasional hypothesis testing is necessary for the counselor to keep his own analytic processes on the track.

Linda: I don't know . . . . More empty but relieved.

Counselor: The resulting sensation is relief and emptiness. Is there a sensation which comes just before that?

Even though his hypothesis does not appear to be immediately validated, the counselor is so convinced that it's correct that he will attempt to test it again.

Linda: Yes . . . anger.

Counselor: So you feel angry. You throw up on Mac. He vanishes and you feel relief.

The counselor again makes a partial summary statement.

Linda: Something like that.

Counselor: Can you let yourself get into that feeling?

This is a curious reply, unless the counselor picked up uneasiness in the client from nonverbal clues or unless he was very sensitive to her hesitancy of response. Yet the counselor's question appears to have been sensitive to a real block that keeps Linda from experiencing, expressing, and relieving her anger.

Linda: No, not really.

Counselor: What seems to be blocking you?

The counselor acknowledges that a block exists and asks if the client is aware of what it is specifically. If the client knows, exploratory time will be saved. Questions can be time savers. If the client knows what is wrong and can tell us, we do not have to go about trying to infer what is wrong from partial cues.

Linda: I don't know. Something is. I can feel myself just keeping it all in . . . mainly protecting myself.

The client does not specifically identify the block but offers the counselor a clue against which he can play a hunch.

Counselor: What you mainly feel yourself doing is keeping the anger in . . . protecting yourself.

The counselor uses a reflective response but changes the client's word "it" to the word "anger."

Linda: Yes.

Counselor: Will you try for a moment to release some of the energy you're spending in protecting yourself? I mean, by actually straightening up right here? (Client straightens up a bit from her hunched position) Now try to allow those angry feelings to come up. (Here the client belches twice.) Allow whatever you feel to come out.

The counselor has observed the client physically acting out her feelings of self-protection. He uses a direct request to get the client to physically represent a less protective posture. She does somewhat. Then the counselor challenges her to get in touch with her angry feelings while in a less protected position. The counselor probably hopes that the client will be able to get more in touch with her blocked feelings as she spends less energy protecting herself. The change of posture may have allowed for the release of accumulated stomach gases, but it's also possible that the presence of stomach gas might be accounted for by stress.

Linda: I can't.

Counselor: What are you experiencing right now?

This and the next counselor response—both questions— urge the client to risk coming in contact with her repressed feelings. This may help break the blocked material or at least indicate the degree of blocking. The counselor is working to specifically identify a cause of his client's problem as well as obtain some indication of how she might behave in the future. The counselor seems to believe that, at least with regard to this boyfriend, the client has a problem in admitting and releasing her anger.

Linda: Panic.

Counselor: Allow yourself to feel this panic. What does it feel like?

Linda: Like if I let everything inside come up, I'll ruin everything. I'll drive him away for good and I'll feel rotten myself.

Counselor: If you release your contained anger you'll destroy any possibility for this relationship and you'll feel responsible for that.

This is another reflective response, except that the counselor substitutes "contained anger" for the client's "everything inside."

Linda: Uh huh. (More tears; client reaches for a Kleenex and blows her nose loudly).

As in her previous comment, the client appears to affirm the counselor's use of the more specific word "anger." The counselor might find it difficult to know if the client's tears are triggered more by the thought that this relationship might end or by her responsibility for ending it. It might become important for the counselor to determine whether the client feels more dismay at the potential loss of this boyfriend or the possible thought that she is a general failure in maintaining relationships.

Counselor: The tears seem to have begun again.

The counselor does not choose at this point to sort out the possible meaning of the tears. Instead he uses a more neutral observation. A question might have been used here to determine the more likely cause of the tears, for example, "Who or what are you crying for?"

Linda: Uh huh.

Counselor: What are you aware of now?

The question seems to indicate that the counselor is using a more cautious approach with the client. The counselor is not playing out hunches in allowing the client to narrate her own awareness.

Linda: I've probably blown it already.

The client indicates a personal sense of responsibility in bringing the relationship with the boyfriend to an end.

Counselor: Somehow you feel that you've sabotaged this relationship yourself.

The counselor underlines this sense of personal responsibility.

Linda: Yes. You see, we still see each other. But now, even when he says he's going to come over, I'm never sure he'll show up. He might call to say he'll be over at 9:00 p.m. and never show up at all—no call, nothing.

The client appears to affirm the counselor's previous statement but also to cloud the issue. Perhaps she wants to let the counselor know that the relationship is not yet over and she is struggling with accepting her own part in the relationship. Or perhaps she wishes simply to draw attention to her boyfriend's behavior. In any case, the client's reply is confusing.

Counselor: Do you feel responsible for his behavior?

The counselor uses a question both to indicate his confusion and to attempt to relieve it.

Linda: Well, I get frantic when he does that and I explode when I see him or . . .

The client seems to pick up on the theme of her responsibility for the present state of her relationship with the boyfriend. She also indicates that she perceives her behavior as reactive and somewhat uncontrollable.

Counselor: You either explode or . . .

Linda: Or I can't take it any more and begin trying to track him down.

Counselor: Can you give an

The counselor again uses a

example of tracking him down?

question to obtain a specific example. It might have been better here for the counselor to have said, "Give an example of tracking him down, please." That way, he would have avoided the chance of the client simply responding "yes" or "no" to what might have seemed like a completely closed question. The danger of this client understanding the counselor's question in a very limited way is minor, given the previous flow of the client-counselor interaction. But in order to avoid some counselor fumbling, should a client respond in an unexpected manner, a direct invitation or or rephrased question is preferred.

Linda: Well, take Tuesday night. He called about 9:00 to say he was on his way over and he *never* showed up. He's never done that before. I began to get frantic. It was the night of that big storm and I thought he might be hurt or something. I started calling hospital emergency rooms and finally about 1:30 a.m. I called his mother. He lives next door to his mother. But he wasn't home. I couldn't sleep after that. So I got up, made a pot of coffee, and went over to his place. It was about 4:30 a.m. He was home by then so I just went in, woke him up, and asked him what he thought he was doing to me. He started to say that

In this narration the client gives evidence of both her persistence in tracking down her boyfriend and of expressing anger toward him.

we'd talk about it tomorrow
—that it was late and all.
But I said we were going to
talk about it right then. He
had kept me up all night
and now he wasn't going to
get any sleep. I was angry
as all get out and I wanted
to see the little twerp suffer.
He straightened up right
quick when he saw how I
was. He said he had met
some friends on the way
over and they had invited
him for a drink. Well, one
thing led to another and he
didn't leave until the bar
closed at 2:00 a.m. I kept
him up till 5:30 a.m. By then
we were both so bummed
out, I left.

Counselor: Let's see what sense I
can make of this. . . . He
stands you up; you get
frantic and, as time goes on,
angry; you track him down
and punish him.

The counselor's response is
pithy. He sequences the client's
events nicely and does not hesi-
tate to say that she was punishing the boyfriend.

Linda: Well, I don't try to get
frantic or angry or anything.
I just can't help myself. All
I can think of is that he's
doing it to me again.

The client suggests again that
she is out of control. Moreover,
she believes the boyfriend is
deliberately doing something
(the vague "it") to her.

Counselor: Here your anger just
blows seemingly without
control.

The counselor chooses to
respond to the client's anger
being out of control. The
counselor could have selected
another response. This perhaps
suggests the counselor's bias
toward the client. How the
counselor chooses to respond,
or what he chooses to respond
to, exert a powerful influence on
the client. The counselor's ability

to influence the client is a positive advantage but should also be a source of caution for the counselor. The counselor must be extremely skilled in the practice of therapy.

Linda: Yes.

Counselor: I'm finding it difficult to understand how at one point you can be afraid to release your contained anger for fear of destroying the very last shreds of your relationship, and at another point can go out of your way to blow up, even punishing him. What am I missing here?

Here the counselor confronts the client with a perceived discrepancy. Notice the delicacy with which the counselor offers the client an out. He does not pin the client in a corner; instead, he suggests he must be missing something in the narration to even perceive a discrepancy.

Linda: Well, Tuesday night I couldn't do anything else. I wasn't even thinking of our relationship, just that he was hurt or that he was doing it to me again. It did cross my mind that he might be with another woman. When I found out he wasn't hurt I just wanted him to feel how I felt. And he did.

The client says that she was not thinking of her relationship with her boyfriend. Instead, she alludes to a different stimulus that accounts for her behavior.

Counselor: I think what you're trying to tell me is that Tuesday night you could not control your anger but when you can, you do.

The counselor's response here is weak but does not appear to interfere with the client's chain of thought. A stronger response, or one directed at obtaining more specific information, might have inhibited the disclosure offered in the next comment.

Linda: You know his behavior just pisses me off, but then I've come to expect that from all men. I mean, he's

Three important disclosures are made here: (1) the client has come to expect personally annoying behavior from most the worst I've ever met, but I don't know many men who feel comfortable in a close relationship or will allow a woman to tell them what to do.

men, (2) few men she has known feel comfortable in close relationships, and (3) few men allow themselves to appear submissive to women.

Counselor: It seems to you that men in general have to a greater or less extent the qualities you dislike in Mac.

The counselor appears to have captured what the client just said, at least in the client's estimation.

Linda: Yes. I can count on the fingers of one hand the number of men I know who are able to enter into an emotional relationship the way a woman can, and they are all in a marriage encounter group.

Counselor: Men and women seem really different to you in this regard. Even the exceptional men have been specially trained.

The counselor is firming up his understanding of the client's communication.

Linda: It's clear as black and white to me.

Counselor: It seems to me that your interactions with Mac are affected by some very deep prejudices in your own background that probably affect your relationships with all men. Unfortunately, we're running out of time so I wonder if we can hold that until later?

The counselor expresses an integrating perception. The counselor here turns on an illuminating light for the client but then apparently fails to allow this to develop in his concern for time.

Linda: Okay.

Counselor: Are you feeling all right enough now to close for today?

The counselor's question expresses caring for the client.

Linda: Yes.

Counselor: Before leaving I'd like to review a few of the points you brought up today. How do you recall the session beginning?

Here the counselor initiates a series of recall questions designed to facilitate the client's remembering material covered from one session to the next.

Linda: I don't know . . . let me see . . . Oh . . . getting into the relationship with Mac.

Counselor: Do you recall feeling that life was playing you a dirty trick independent of anything you did?

Linda: Yes.

Counselor: Do you feel the same way right now?

The counselor is checking for client movement during this session through the use of a question.

Linda: Not exactly; I seem to have some input.

Counselor: What do you recall next?

Linda: Feeling hit, hurt.

Counselor: Feeling hit, hurt, and self-protective. Do you also recall wanting to throw up on Mac?

Here we see a reflective response expanded by the inclusion of "self-protective" followed by a recall question.

Linda: Yes, but not able to.

Counselor: Not able to because you might completely destroy your relationship with him if you released your anger. What else do you recall?

The counselor puts into words previously implied material.

Linda: How lousy he treated me Tuesday.

Counselor: And what about your behavior?

The counselor uses a question to direct the client's focus of attention to her own behavior.

Linda: And how I felt so frantic I had to find him.

Counselor: You felt frantic, found him, and punished him. You were angry and you expressed it in no uncertain terms.

The direct confrontation is couched in terms of previously mentioned material

Linda: But I couldn't help it.

The client seems to defend herself.

Counelor: You felt out of control and therefore not responsible. Is there anything else you can recall?

Linda: No, I think that's all.

Counselor: What about expecting "Mac-like" behavior from most men?

The counselor continues to use questions to cover all the main points of the interview in recall.

Linda: Yeah, I do. I've never had many other examples in my life. I seem mainly to end up with guys like Mac. Although he's the worst and the one I'm most hooked on.

The client adds some new material here.

Counselor: You also mentioned that you felt somehow you had sabotaged this relationship. What about that?

The counselor chooses not to respond to this material at this point; instead, he focuses more attention on the client's perceived role in her relationship with her boyfriend.

Linda: Well . . . I feel that at least I have something to do with where it is right now. Though how much I don't know.

The client appears more ready to accept her part in the development of this relationship. A positive step in treatment.

Counselor: That might be a point of departure until our next session.

POSTSCRIPT

The analysis of the counselor's dialogue in the two transcripts is probably the best method of evaluating your own actual counseling sessions. If you can determine the purpose and rationale for each response you make to the client, you are well on your way to being a competent and effective counselor. Admittedly, it is quite difficult to have access to typed transcripts of every counseling session. This is why audiotaping is encouraged whenever possible. It is precisely this type of analysis and evaluation that contributes to your ability to understand and react appropriately to the responses of the client.

The two transcripts not only demonstrate that the counselors were using questions appropriately, but also that the basic objectives of each phase of the process were being achieved, not by trial and error but by the planned verbal and nonverbal interaction of the counselor.

8

The Structured
Interview

There is no greater time when the appropriate use of questions is more crucial than in the *structured interview*. In this chapter, the various types of questions that have been discussed previously will be examined in the context of the structured interview.

Most counselors, whether they work in school or agency settings, are called upon at some point to conduct a structured interview. When counselors are familiar with the nature and purpose of structured interviews, their effectiveness is maximized. Structured interviewing is essentially different from counseling and it can be difficult to keep these differences in perspective.

STRUCTURED INTERVIEW: NATURE AND PURPOSE

A structured interview exists whenever there is a well planned and explicit procedural outline for the dialogue between the client and the counselor. This can range from a simple list of questions to be answered by the client to an entire case history evaluation for which several hours of inquiry are necessary. Structured interviews include the commonly used in-take interview and the mental status examination. In-take interviews are relatively standard procedures in agency counseling activities; mental status examinations are found more exclusively in psychiatric settings. Later in this chapter we'll present models for questions that characterize each type of structured interview.

In the structured interview, the counselor has responsibility for the direction and course of the interview. The areas to be covered include predetermined information that needs to be acquired from the interview. This is quite different from the counselor's role in a standard counseling interview, where responsibility does not rest entirely with the counselor. Indeed, as Rogers (1951) and later proponents of his humanistic approach, (Carkhuff, 1969a; Carkhuff & Berenson, 1977; Egan, 1975) to counseling suggest, the client decides not only what will be discussed but also the ultimate direction of the interview.

This is not to say that structured interviews are not or cannot be part of the standard counseling process. Indeed, in the majority of helping situations, structured interviews *are* a part of the overall helping process. They generally provide the necessary information from which to begin some sort of initial helping role.

For example, this can occur when an employment counselor is obtaining information needed to help a person with a vocational problem; when a social worker or family counselor interviews a married couple or family; when a school counselor interviews parents in a school-related problem; when an agency counselor does an in-take interview to determine the problem and obtain information to help a client in distress; or when a crisis intervention counselor acquires information about a client as quickly as possible to effectively help in the crisis.

The primary purpose of the structured interview is to obtain necessary *a priori* information to provide effective help. Obtaining needed information is best accomplished this way because it is the fastest method possible. Alternatively, counseling could begin and information to answer necessary questions could develop while counseling was taking place, but this would probably be counterproductive to the overall helping effort.

For example, counselors working in community mental health agencies are generally required to perform a formal in-take interview, wherein needed information is obtained to help determine a diagnosis and direction of the counseling or therapy intervention strategies. The information is generally required before any therapeutic effort is undertaken. The same situation is also true for counselors working in other settings, whether it be a college counseling center or an elementary or secondary school setting. The structured interview can provide a rich source of data on the past, present, and future of a client in much the same way as do data from psychological and ability tests—only much more accurately and therapeutically. This information can usually be obtained by a lengthy form or questionnaire, but an interview is always preferable for several reasons:

1. Clients should feel that they are being taken care of by someone who wants to help them. Having clients fill out elaborate and detailed forms only exacerbates their problem and encourages negative feelings between the client and the helping agency.
2. The interviewer can allow the client to expand and explore other issues relevant to the information being obtained. This can be done

without transforming the structured interview into a counseling session.

3. The interviewer can begin to understand the client and his or her perceptions of the problems in addition to acquiring important information by making careful observations of how and what was answered by the questions. This observational information has considerable value in understanding the client and cannot be obtained by simply answering questions on a form or questionnaire. For example, the interviewer can see the client's general intellectual level by noting not only the stated level of education but also observing the method and manner of the client's responses—the client's level of comprehension and vocabulary. This information can be very important in later therapeutic efforts.

4. Perhaps most important, the interviewer can observe the client's overall behavior, exclusive of what is being discussed. Enelow and Wexler (1966) call this the *process of the structured interview*. These observations include such aspects of the client's behavior as tension and anxiety in voice, speech, and nonverbal behaviors. With this discrimination between the process (how things occurred during the interview) and content (what the client talked about), Enelow and Wexler divide the structured interview into two components of information: process and content. While the counselor is not always concerned with process in a structured interview, it is always advisable to make observations that can later be useful in counseling. For example, if the client becomes overtly anxious and stutters and stammers whenever he or she discusses the father, it would be useful to note this for later counseling.

Restated, both *what* is said and *how* it is said, together with observations made during the structured interview, should be noted because this type of *information* can provide additional insight into later therapeutic efforts. Organizing the interview information into Enelow and Wexler's two components can help provide an overall picture of the situation and facilitate further understanding of the client's problem. An example can best illustrate this point.

The Case of Mrs. W.

Mrs. W. is a 40-year-old housewife, mother of two children, who describes herself as having problems finding employment. Her general appearance at the time of the interview was somewhat unkempt and sloppy. Mrs. W. describes herself as not having any interest or motivation in household activities she had previously enjoyed. She has a bachelor's degree in teaching, but married shortly after college and has never had a job. She recalled with some sadness the pleasure of being home with her children until they grew up and left home. It was then that she realized she needed additional activities to occupy her time. Yet she has failed in all of her efforts to find employment, and she gave examples to show that this was when she started feeling inadequate and self-deprecative. She further stated that she now feels it is her fault because she has nothing to offer anyone, and feels worthless much of the time. She recounted being so tense before any job interview that she could not present herself as anything other than a "scatterbrain," and subsequently no one would hire her. Throughout the interview, Mrs. W.'s voice quivered with anxiety. Her eye contact was poor, especially when she was talking about herself.

Analysis of Interview.

Process	*Content*
1. Tension in voice	1. Forty-year-old mother of two and housewife
2. Sloppy appearance	2. Unhappy in current situation
3. Sadness in speech at key points	3. Inability to find meaningful activities or job
4. Poor eye contact	4. Self-deprecating feelings and behaviors

Analyzing the interview this way will help provide a systematic organization of the information from your questions. Organization of the information into process and content components may not provide any answers, but as Maloney and Ward (1976) suggest, it can facilitate understanding the overall picture of an individual's problem and suggest additional questions for further inquiry and greater understanding.

THE CONDUCT OF STRUCTURED INTERVIEWS

As mentioned above, the structured interview is conducted somewhat differently from the counseling interview. Whereas the counseling interview seeks to develop a therapeutic relationship and provide help to the client, the structured interview attempts to develop a brief overview of the client's problem and the context in which that problem is occurring. Below are comparisons between structured interviews and counseling interviews.

Obtaining Information versus Therapeutic Helping. Structured interviews and counseling interviews differ most obviously in their basic purpose. Structured interviews are used to obtain initial information about the client, the presenting problem, and the context in which the problem occurs. This information, usually obtained during the first or in-take session, is used to plan and develop the most appropriate intervention strategies as well as the general therapeutic handling of the client.

In contrast, the major purpose of the counseling interview is to provide the helping strategies to assist the client in attaining his or her counseling goals and objectives.

This is a relatively difficult discrimination for most beginning counselors to make, since obtaining information is generally a part of the counseling interview; but counseling *per se* is seldom part of the structured interview. As a result, the tendency on the part of the counselor is to begin counseling during a structured interview.

It should be noted that getting into counseling during the structured interview will only detract and prolong the initial in-take period. In addition, the in-take interviewer may not be the person doing the counseling; thus, the initial counseling efforts may be wasted therapeutic time. This is not to say that initial structured interviews shouldn't be empathic and helpful. Conveying empathy and a genuine desire to help are essential to effective counseling. The initial structured interview, regardless of how detailed it is or who actually conducts it, is the first step in the total therapeutic process. Demonstrating that help is available for the client will greatly facilitate the goals of the structured interview. The client's first impressions can be lasting ones.

Empathy and Demonstrated Helpfulness. Empathy and demonstrated helpfulness are essential to the counseling interviews as well as the structured interview. In most cases, the initial or in-take interview will be the first contact with the client. It is essential that the same caring and level of empathy expected for later counseling are present during the structured interview. Clients will be more open when they feel questions have a legitimate purpose and that the interviewer is genuinely concerned about their well-being.

It is very easy to rush through a long list of questions in a cold and mechanical manner. This is the very same danger that exists in using any predetermined list of questions. There is always a risk that questions will degenerate into judgmental and mechanical responses that can foster defensiveness and counterproductive feelings in the client. This is why interviewers should monitor their questioning behavior throughout structured interviews to ensure that they are being sensitive to the client while they complete their list of questions. If there isn't enough time to get the information needed, schedule another session to complete the questions. Do not attempt to hurry through the interview.

A Preplanned Format. In the structured interview, a preplanned format is essential to obtaining the appropriate information in a professional manner. The areas of inquiry—presenting the problem, description of onset, family history, etc.—should be carefully delineated before the interview to ensure the effectiveness of the questions and to minimize the amount of time used before counseling begins. Structured interviews at the beginning of counseling consume both time and client resources, so it is important to keep all initial efforts as short as possible.

During the counseling interview, the counselor will probably not be able to follow a specific preplanned format, since the exact direction of the sessions are determined by counselor-client interaction during the process. Later in this chapter, we will present a standard preplanned format for the structured interview representative of the appropriate use of questions.

Getting Side-Tracked.   It is important in the structured interview to stay with the topics of inquiry. Because of the nature of the questions, clients will often stray from the information being sought. This should be avoided, as it is time consuming and not productive in the initial interview. There are times, however, when deviation from the format of questions can be considerably productive. The in-take interviewer should decide whether to let the client continue or to bring him or her back to the topic at hand. The decision should be based on whether the information is essential to the in-take process or just tangential, "nice-to-know" information. If it can't hurt, but it also can't help, then valuable therapeutic time is being wasted. The client may feel that he or she is actually getting into the counseling process when this is really not occurring. The client may end up having to repeat the same information to the counselor, and this may not facilitate the counseling process. In fact, this may prove to be counterproductive to the client's desire to obtain immediate assistance with a problem.

Getting side-tracked on issues the client elaborates on *can* be beneficial; in many approaches to counseling it is encouraged. Allowing the client to focus or expand on issues he or she feels are important is an excellent way to facilitate the counseling process.

On the other hand, in both structured interviews and counseling interviews, frequent side-tracking can be a sign of the client's avoidance of certain topics. If any consistent patterns of side-tracking are observed by the interviewer, they should be noted.

Getting the client back to the format of the interview is done by simply interrupting with the next question. If done smoothly, it should have little negative effect. If this must be done repeatedly throughout an interiew, the interviewer may want to mildly confront the client with the need to continue the questions, since the interview time is quickly drawing to a close. For example,

Dennis: . . . and another thing happened then that I thought was significant . . .

Mr. Piper: Let me ask you another question about when you first started to notice this problem.

Or

Mr. Piper: We'd better press on with these questions we need to cover first. So let me ask you about . . .

Or

Mr. Piper: I think your counselor would be interested in that. It might be better if you waited rather than get into it now. But I do want to ask you if . . .

Or

Mr. Piper: Forgive me if there are a lot of different aspects of your situation we have to cover hurriedly. There'll be more time for you to talk about these things in greater detail after we finish these questions. For now, let me get back to . . .

Generally, a mild confrontation or explanation of the purpose of the interview should suffice to keep the client on track and aid the interviewer in completing the questions.

Counsel in a Counseling Interview; Don't Counsel in a Structured Interview.   There are times when interviews with preplanned questions can take three to five sessions because the interviewers accidentally slip into counseling roles. The lesson is this: Don't counsel when doing structured interviews and, likewise, don't interview when doing counseling.

Counseling during the structured interview only slows the entire process. The interviewer will not always be the counselor, so the client has to repeat what was said already. In most cases, the interviewer will only have time to obtain answers to the preplanned questions.

When both client and counselor are aware of the basic purposes of the structured interview and how they differ from the counseling interview, the tendency to confuse the two is greatly minimized. It is always good to inform the client at the onset of the purpose of the structured interview. Explain that while many of the questions may seem to be unrelated to the specific problem presented, the information will be useful in helping the staff plan the best possible help.

Additionally, tell the client that all information provided will be treated confidentially in accordance with the agency's standard operating procedures and the profession's ethical code. This should encourage the client to be as open and candid as possible. An example can best illustrate this:

Counselor: Hello, Mr. Goulet, I'm Leon M. and I'll be talking to you about your coming here to _____. I've got a number of questions I'd like to ask you that will help us plan how best we can help you. Some of these may seem a little unrelated to your present situation, but they can be very helpful to us in helping you. Do you have any questions?

Client: Well, about how long will this take and when do I see a counselor?

Counselor: This should only take about 30-45 minutes. I'll give the information to our staff, and the next time you come in you'll see the person who'll be your counselor. I should also mention that what we talk about will be confidential between you and our staff. Is there anything else I can explain?

This allows the interviewer to clarify any problems or misconceptions about the initial interview. It will also clarify the counseling process if the client requests additional information or the interviewer feels clarification is required.

The Use of Note Taking.   It is generally a good idea to have the questions you're going to ask with you, so that taking notes during the structured interview is easy. It is also encouraged to ensure the accuracy of both the information obtained and the observations, if any, that were made. This is in direct contrast to counseling interviews, where note-taking is *discouraged* because it interferes with the attention of the client, who focuses on what the counselor is writing down. In fact, taking notes reinforces inappropriate verbal responses because the client feels that what was said must be important if the counselor is writing it down. Most counseling approaches highly discourage the practice of taking notes during the session.

In the structured interview, however, note taking is often necessary. Even if the session is being taped, it is advisable to have the questions before you to record any observations that would not be available from an audiotape recording.

The use of note-taking can also help to keep the client from getting side-tracked on tangential issues. For example,

Counselor: Mr. Barker, could you tell me again those three things that you just mentioned?

Or

Counselor: Let me make sure I have all of this down. Could we go back to what you said earlier about your boss?

This will refocus the client to the questions being asked and should help prevent getting side-tracked.

In sum, counseling interviews are different from structured interviews. Their purposes will be better served if both client and counselor are aware of this. Remember their main differences:

Structured Interview	*Counseling Interview*
Obtaining information	Therapeutic helping
Empathy and demonstrated helpfulness	Empathy and demonstrated helpfulness
Preplanned format	Format not preplanned
Counselor primarily responsible for conduct of interviews	Mutual responsibility for conduct of interview
Avoidance of client side-tracking	Client side-tracking may be relevant
Don't counsel, interview	Don't interview, counsel
Take notes	Never take notes
Make relevant observations	Make relevant observations

TYPES OF QUESTIONS

Depending on the amount and depth of information being sought, all of the various types of questions discussed in earlier chapters are used in the structured interview. The open-ended and the direct question serve additional functions.

The Open-Ended Question

The open-ended question, as you'll remember, requires the client to respond with more information than a simple "yes" or "no" answer. It is exceptionally useful in structured interviews because the client is free to respond in any way he or she wishes. A question such as, "Would you tell me something about your parents?" or "Could you tell me more about what has brought you to see me?" allows the client to begin anywhere and respond in any way he or she desires. In a somewhat contradictory sense, this is an unstructured way to obtain structured information.

Open-ended questions are probably the most prevalent type of question asked, for they afford the interviewer an opportunity to observe how the client reacts. Using open-ended questions to inquire about significant topical areas provides observational information relevant to the latency of clients' responses, their speech patterns, vocabulary, logic and completeness of thought, and degree of anxiety (Maloney & Ward, 1976). All these variables may play a role in the overall assessment of the information obtained.

Thus, open-ended questions allow the client to expand and self-disclose to the extent he or she feels comfortable. This can be quite useful whenever the interviewer is unsure of how far to expand on a given issue. And finally, as we discussed in earlier chapters, the open-ended question can help to facilitate client self-disclosure. With nonverbal clients this can be an asset to obtaining the needed information with considerably fewer questions.

Direct Questions

Generally, where specific information is required or when follow-up information to an open-ended question is necessary, the direct question is most useful.

Occasionally, the direct question can be a useful technique to limit the amount of information in a client's response, especially if the client tends to ramble or be long-winded. It can also be used effectively to interrupt the client and refocus the response to the original question. For example:

Mr. Jenkins: So I went to see my friend who owns a shoeshine parlor.

Mrs. Lynch: Mr. Jenkins, when did you realize that other people were noticing your fear?

Direct questions can also be used toward the end of the session to complete any unanswered questions that occur during the course of the interview. An interviewer can make the following responses:

Before we stop, I have several questions that we haven't covered yet. How many children are at home with you? Are you on any medication from a physician? [and so on]

STRUCTURED INTERVIEW FORMAT

In the structured interview, the questions are based upon the type of information to be obtained. Different counseling situations will require different amounts of initial information from the client. Additionally, each agency may have its own format for the conduct of structured or initial interviews.

In this section, we will present a general format for structured interviews together with examples of complete and detailed questions. For many counseling situations, this level of completeness and detail will not be necessary. The counselor should edit and modify the questions based on progress of the individual interview.

Presenting Problems

Generally, the single most important area of inquiry is the reason or purpose for the client's coming to a counselor. It should therefore be the area in which information is first obtained. While the presenting problem may not be the client's *real* problem—or while the client may not even be able to define the problem—the issue or concern the client does present should be addressed before any others.

Inquiring about the presenting problem can best be accomplished by open-ended questions. This will encourage the client to begin talking about the problem in general terms and allow for follow-up questions that are more specific in nature.

Additionally, it is essential to determine what the person wants out of counseling—what he or she would hope to gain and how he or she would like to see the problem resolved. Questions of this type will help to clarify any initial misconceptions or unwarranted expectations that could be counterproductive to the helping process. It will also help build from the start a realistic impression of what counseling is all about and what the client's role will be in this process. If these issues are handled during the initial interview, later counseling efforts will be maximized.

General
Can you tell me about what brings you here, Mrs. R.?
What is it, Mr. C., that we can help you with?
Maybe you could tell me about what's been troubling you.

Specific
Can you elaborate on these headaches that you've been having?
How long has this situation been going on?
When did you first notice these feelings?
Can you think back and try to remember if there was anything else
    significant that happened about the same time as this?
How has this problem been affecting the other areas of your life?

During this phase of the structured interview, it is essential to ascertain the important elements of the person's problem, to demonstrate empathy and to indicate that help can be provided. It is also important, especially when the client is describing the problem, not to actually counsel the individual. It is very easy to inadvertently begin counseling during this phase of the interview.

Family History

Information on the family history of the client may or may not be directly relevant to the presenting problem; however, it is useful to know certain facts of the client's family history in order to have some understanding of the person. The amount of detail required may vary considerably and should be based on the nature of the problem that is initially presented by the client. Pieces of family history information will also be obtained throughout the course of the interview without direct inquiry.

Nonetheless, some type of preplanned checklist will ensure that no pertinent information is overlooked. Topics under family history should include:

Family background
Number of siblings
Any relatives who are living in the home presently or in the past
Quality of relationships with parents, brothers, sisters, wife, children, and so on
A general description of the climate within the family
Effects of presenting problem on the client's family life
Any additional demographic characteristics that may be mentioned by the client in response to these areas

Typical questions might include:

Could you tell me a little about your present family situation?
Could you describe your relationship with your wife, children, parents, and so on?
How has this problem affected your family?
What kinds of things do you remember about growing up?
How many brothers and sisters do you have and what are their ages?

Once again, open-ended questions will be the most facilitative and most frequently used. Direct questions used to obtain specific or follow-up information to open-ended questions will also contribute to family history information.

Personal History

Personal history entails information about the client's own development as he or she perceives it. Questions used to elicit information about this category may or may not be directly relevant to the client's presenting problem. Initiation of questions dealing with the client's development may at times be perceived as attempts to uncover subtle causes and explanations from out of the past. This should be cautiously avoided; we suggest that only information relevant to the presenting problem be sought at this stage of the interview.

It should be re-emphasized that an overemphasis of information from the past will provide little verifiable or useful insight to a valid counseling solution or treatment recommendation. It is more useful to focus on aspects of personal development that the client reports as having significant impact upon the present situation. With this in mind, personal development can be divided into four main areas of inquiry:

1. Infancy
2. Childhood

3. Adolescence
4. Adulthood

Depending on the nature of the information required, early developmental periods may be de-emphasized and later periods may be more focused. Typical areas of inquiry include the following:

1. *Infancy*
   Presence or absence of parents and siblings in the home
   Significant milestones or developmental problems
   Illnesses or injuries
   Recollections of childhood experiences
2. *Childhood*
   Recollections of preschool and school years
   Development of childhood relationships
   Issues related to childhood activities; for example, friends, clubs, hobbies, etc.
   Parental discipline
   School achievement and ability
3. *Adolescence*
   Social, emotional, and academic adjustment; for example, dating, relationships with parents, etc.
   School activities
   Development of career and life goals
   Significant events during this period
4. *Adulthood*
   Family relationships
   Career plans and efforts including jobs, training, and schooling
   Significant events related to adult life

   Typical questions might include:

Could you tell me about anything you remember or were told about your infancy?
What were the significant events that you can remember during your years growing up?
What types of memories do you have about your parents?
What are some pleasant and unpleasant experiences you remember about your school years?
Tell me about how you get along with your brothers and sisters now? Is that different from when you were growing up?
Would you tell me a little about your married life?
What kinds of things do you do for recreation?
Could you describe how you feel about the way your life has worked out?

Some of the information in this area will not be directly relevant to the client's problem or present situation, and it is extremely time consuming to collect in a comprehensive way. This is why interviewers are encouraged to decide the types of information that will be relevant on the basis of the person and the presenting problems and to use that as a template to question significant elements of the individual's personal history.

As mentioned earlier, it is always better to question information that the client has identified as significant in his or her personal history rather than to probe for possible underlying elements. If the interviewer, by using open-ended questions, allows the client to freely discuss his or her personal history, significant information should come to the forefront. Also, the amount of time allowable to question life-span development may be quite limited. Generally speaking, where time is a consideration, the historical data, personal history, and family history can be de-emphasized so that the presenting problem and the context in which it occurs receives the greatest attention.

MENTAL STATUS

While structured interviews are not conducted to make a psychological or psychiatric diagnosis, it is usually beneficial to make some preliminary judgments about the individual's current mental status during the interview. The information can be quite useful in planning for future treatment interventions, especially when the counselor suspects that severe psychopathology may be present.

If the presence of psychopathology is a consideration, the mental status exam may be useful in differentiating the severity of the disturbance. Making a judgment between the presence of a counseling problem and a psychiatric problem is called a *differential diagnosis*, and may be a critical judgment for the interviewer during initial client contacts.

For clients who have demonstrable impairments, problems with reality, disorientation, and so forth, the judgments made can affect the decision of treatment modality as well as suggest further diagnostic evaluations—all essential to appropriate helping efforts.

It should be noted that while questions will provide significant information about the client's mental status, observation by the interviewer will also contribute heavily to the overall information provided.

Content Areas to Consider

The content areas presented below are based on the work of Crary and Johnson (1975), and are abstracted to include those areas of significant interest to counselors and mental health workers involved in initial structured interviews. They should not be considered sufficient in scope and content to base a diagnosis, but rather are gross indications that further evaluation and information may be required in order to plan and implement successful treatment strategies.

1. Appearance. Consideration should be given to how the individual presents him- or herself at the time of the interview. Is it appropriate for his or her age, social position, and so forth? Remember, however, that general appearance is a crude benchmark to indicate the level of a person's problem and the impact it has on physical functioning, yet where there appear to be inconsistencies, inquiries should be made. As Maloney and Ward (1976) suggest, "Marked changes in dress and personal hygiene are often associated with psychological disturbance, particularly when severe" (p. 92).

Questions such as, "How has this problem affected your personal functioning?" or "Have you noticed any changes in your overall health or appearance since this problem began?" will help to gain an understanding of the personal ramifications of the problem.

2. Behavior. This includes the verbal and nonverbal behavior of the individual throughout the course of the interview. Observations made about the client's behavior will be useful in determining the content and process elements of the interview that were discussed earlier.

Where verbal and nonverbal behavior seem to be significant, follow-up questions can be asked to further clarify their importance. For example, "Mr. Smith, I've noticed that you've been biting your nails throughout our talk. Is this something you've always done?" or "You seem very tired, Ms. Webster; have you noticed yourself being tired more since this problem has been troubling you?

Possible topical areas of inquiry into behavior may include the following verbal and nonverbal behaviors:

Verbal
Speech
Tone of voice
Excitability of voice
Stuttering or stammering, rapidity of speech
General responses to questions

Nonverbal
Eye contact, especially when significant areas are questioned
Mood and affect; that is, smiles, laughs, frowns, facial expressions, when inappropriate to the content being discussed
Nervous mannerisms; for example, finger or foot tapping, nail-biting, fidgety behaviors
Body posture

Typical questions might include:

You seem to be under a lot of pressure when you talk. Have you noticed that effect on you?
How has this problem affected your general mood?
Are you aware that you seem extremely fidgety?
How long has the stammering in your voice been present?
Is it upsetting to you when you think about what you have just said?
Is it difficult to talk about these things?

Sensorium and General Level of Intellectual Processes

The individual's general level of sensory and intellectual functioning is an essential element in the determination of potential for and type of treatment, severity of problem, and general degree of impairment relative to the problem. Client-interviewer interactions throughout the course of an initial interview can provide a good indication of a client's sensory and intellectual functioning. However, depending on the severity and impact of the problem, it may be necessary to make some initial screening judgments. These judgments will enhance the overall determination of the type and extent of the helping process.

Eaton and Peterson (1969) present a comprehensive examination of the factors that comprise this area. They suggest the specific evaluation of this area whenever confusion, intellectual deficit, or possible neurological problems are present. In most cases, however, the interviewer can make preliminary evaluations where needed to suggest further analysis. The following areas are generally included whenever an evaluation of sensorium and intellectual functioning are part of the interviewer's task:

Orientation.   Is the client oriented to person, place, and time? That is, is the client aware of who he or she is, where he or she is, and what time it is (date, time of day)? Under most circumstances, orientation of the client will be obvious and questioning will not be needed to establish this. Disorientation generally suggests severe problems, especially where the client's disorientation involves the sense of self. Simple questions can establish orientation when needed. For example:

Can you tell me who you are and what you do for a living?
How did you get here?
Do you know where you are?
Can you tell me what season this is and what today's date is?

Once again, extreme disorientation can be indicative of severe problems—either physical or emotional—and is suggestive of additional evaluation efforts.

Memory.   Questioning on memory is usually divided into imme-diate, recent, and remote memory. Disturbances in memory can be indicative of severe problems. Assessing the three areas of memory can be accomplished by questions related to significant events in the indi-vidual's life or by recall of prominent historical or current events. For example.

Can you tell me your social security number, phone number, and birthday?
Can you remember the approximate dates of World War II?
Do you remember the name of this agency?
Do you recall the name of the high school you went to?
Do you remember the first automobile you owned?
Do you recall who the Mayor is? the President?
Do you remember your mother's maiden name?

Arithmetic Ability.   Eaton and Peterson (1969) suggest that rote memory, auditory memory, and arithmetic ability can be checked by asking the client to repeat a series of digits or by giving the client simple problems and calculations to do. This type of inquiry can provide further information about the client's memory and overall mental func-tioning by means of a series of simple questions. For example:

Can you repeat these digits, 5 - 4 - 3 - 7 - 2 - 9 (pausing about a second between each one and increasing the number of digits if necessary)?
Would you start at 100 and subtract 3 from each number and continue doing this? For example, 100 - 97 - 94. Can you continue from there?
Can you divide 12 by 3 and multiply the answer by 2?

Conceptual, Concrete, and Abstract Thinking.   Evidence from educational training and experience may provide sufficient information about the conceptual level of the client. If further information is required about the level of abstract/concrete thinking, the interpretation of the meaning of several proverbs may be useful. This is a common approach used by several intelligence tests and will provide sufficient insight in thinking levels. For example:

Can you tell me what the expression "Empty wagons make the most noise" means?
Can you tell me what it means when you say, "A stitch in time saves nine?"

The client's response to these proverbs—whether they're concrete and specific, or abstract and general—should provide a strong indication of his or her ability at abstract thinking.

Judgment. This refers to a person's ability to make appropriate decisions and carry out the day-to-day activities of living. Assessments relating to the nature of the client's judgment can usually be made from the information provided during the interview. When additional information is required, it can be obtained by asking the client to relate a problem-solving activity or experience. For example:

Can you tell me how you decided to get into the line of work you are in?
Can you tell me how you came to decide to come to this counseling center?
What kinds of things would you do if you wanted to buy a house to ensure you weren't being cheated?

With questions of this type, the interviewer should be cognizant of the reasoning and analysis of the problem as well as the speed with which responses are provided.

Insight. Some general assessment of the client's level of awareness toward his or her situation and problem should be undertaken. The assessment of the client's insight can have considerable implications for the type of help offered. The main area of focus should be on the individual's ability to verbalize the problem and its ramifications on his or her life situation. This can be done primarily when the client is discussing the nature of the presenting problem. If more information is necessary, the interviewer may return to this area of inquiry for additional questions. For example, "Let's go back to the reason you're here. Can you tell me more about how this problem has affected your relationship with your family?"

Perceptual Processes. Perceptual processes refer to the five senses of seeing, hearing, smelling, tasting, and touching. If the interviewer suspects the presence of any perceptual difficulties or hallucinations, questions should address these areas. For example: "I'm wondering if you ever have any experiences involving seeing or hearing things that seem strange or unexplainable?" You may want to avoid using the term "hallucination" because of its strong pejorative connotation, unless the individual initiates use of the word.

Demeanor and Affect. These terms generally apply to the client's overall emotional state during the interview. This assessment is generally accomplished by observation and includes such areas as:

The client's reaction to questions
The level of cooperation or resistance to the interview
Verbal and nonverbal expressions of feeling; for example, anger, sorrow, grief, elation

Appropriateness of affect to the content being discussed (Crying when one should be happy, and the reverse, can be an important sign of difficulties and should be pursued with follow-up questions.)
Overall motivation for help
Inquiries into thoughts of suicide

If during the interview additional information relevant to demeanor or affect is necessary, you can ask questions in the following form:

Can you tell me your reasons for feeling so negative about the whole experience?
Are you aware that when you were discussing that you seemed to be smiling at the whole event?
How do you feel about being asked all these questions?
Are you aware that you appear reluctant in responding to questions about the problem?
I was wondering if you could tell me about any thoughts of suicide you may have had.

These areas comprise a relatively complete format from which to make some initial judgments about the client's current mental functioning. Information from these areas will be useful in providing an understanding of the client and contribute greatly to the overall goal of the structured interview: to provide information about the client, the problem, and the context in which the problem occurs.

Obviously, inclusion of specific mental status questions will add considerably to the total amount of time required to conduct the interview. You should judge which dimensions of the mental status segment should be included. Once again, however, this judgment will usually be based on the completeness that is required for each initial interview.

While most interviewers may not choose to address each area in detail, they should nonetheless be aware of the various areas and make observations relevant to these areas throughout the interview. Any impressions, especially when based upon follow-up information of mental status will provide beneficial information for the determination of the most meaningful and productive course for helping.

SUMMARY

The structured interview attempts to gain information about the client, the problem, and the context in which the problem is occurring. It is a well planned attempt by the interviewer to structure the types of information and dialogue that will occur, in order to provide information essential to the determination of the best treatment or helping approach for each client. This task is primarily accomplished by the use of questions. The following is an outline of the relevant areas of inquiry for the structured interview.

I. Presenting problem
   A. Description of problem
   B. Impact of problem upon individual functioning
II. Reasons for coming to counseling
   A. Motivation for help
   B. How client would like problem resolved
   C. Perceptions and expectations for and about the counseling process
III. Family history
   A. Background
   B. Relationships with parents and siblings
   C. General family life
IV. Personal history
   A. Infancy
   B. Childhood
   C. Adolescence
   D. Adulthood
V. Mental status
   A. Appearance
   B. Behavior
      1. Verbal
      2. Nonverbal
   C. Sensorium and general level of intellectual processes
      1. Memory
      2. Arithmetic Ability
      3. Conceptual
      4. Judgment
      5. Insight
      6. Perpectual Processes
      7. Demeanor and Affect
VI. Observations. It should also be emphasized that significant observations and impressions from the interview should be noted. These generally include:
   A. appearance
   B. demeanor and affect
   C. prevalent verbal and nonverbal behaviors
   D. anxiety or nervous behavior
   E. presence of appropriate affect
   F. general degree of cooperation
   G. overall responsiveness to the questions

The outline presented above can serve as a checklist, when relevant questions are added to each section. It should be kept in mind that the use of questions in the structured interview should not be undertaken in a mechanistic, impersonal manner, but rather with the qualities of empathy and helpfulness to demonstrate that the interviewer's purpose is to be of help and concern for the problems facing the client.

EXERCISES

In the following two case studies, identify the process and content of each in the spaces provided. After the two cases have been completed, look over the components of each and try to develop a clear picture of who the person is, the presenting problem, the context in which the problem occurs, and any additional questions you would like to ask as well as recommendations you may have about possible therapeutic efforts for each case. Possible solutions can be found on page 256.

The Case of Don L.

Don is a 20-year-old college junior who appears to be bright and quite proud of his academic achievements. Don's appearance is neat and his physical features suggest a person younger than his years. Don is somewhat evasive as to his reasons for seeking counseling at first, but later some comments suggestive of homosexuality indicate that this was the reason for coming to the counseling center. However, throughout the entire first interview, this admission is the only specific mention of homosexuality. Don would subsequently refer to these feelings as "this problem," or "this thing," his voice reflecting tension and hesitation whenever reference to homosexuality was made. Don reports that he had no close relationships with women during his adolescence, with minimal physical contact to encourage heterosexual feelings. He emphasized that he has been depressed about his homosexual feelings, stating that he has tried every way he knew to change, but nothing has worked. All indications suggest that he seems to be sincere in his desire to change and he sees counseling as the way to "make him change."

1. *Process*

_____

_____

_____

_____

_____

_____

2. *Content*

_____

_____

_____

_____

_____

_____

3. This person is (describe him) _____

_____

_____

4. His presenting problem is _____

_____

_____

5. The context in which the presenting problem is occurring is ____

_____

_____

_____

6. What additional questions would you ask him? _____

_____

_____

_____

7. Recommendations: _____

_____

_____

The Case of Mrs. B.

Mrs. B. is a 45-year-old housewife, mother of two teenage sons and a teenage daughter. She reports that her marriage is very good and that there are no problems in her relationship with her husband. Her appearance is neat and she is well dressed. Mrs. B. first reported that lately everything seems to bother her, but as she explained this further, she became more specific, stating that she has lost control over her children. She complained that she has not been able to enforce any degree of discipline or respect on her sons, who frequently ridicule her efforts to control their behavior. She also mentioned extreme upset because she suspects her daughter is having sexual relations with a boy she dates. Mrs. B. reports shock and dismay with this situation, stating that she feels sex outside of marriage is wrong and she has a right to know the details of her daughter's dating activities. Her eye contact was very good throughout the interview, but the topic of sex caused her to look at the floor whenever she discussed anything related to her daughter's dating or her own strong religious beliefs. Mrs. B. reports that she was raised in a strict religious home and she has always felt the necessity of passing on a strict moral code to her children. She blames herself for failing to be the kind of mother her own mother was. She wants help to be able to re-establish the necessary control over her children before something terrible happens.

1. *Process*

_____

_____

_____

_____

_____

_____

2. *Content*

_____

_____

_____

_____

_____

3. This person is (describe her) _____

_____

_____

4. Her presenting problem is _____

_____

_____

5. The context in which the presenting problem is occurring is _____

_____

_____

_____

6. What additional question would you like to ask her? _____

_____

_____

_____

7. Recommendations: _____

_____

_____

Possible Solutions

Don L.
Process:
1. High value on performance in school
2. Youthful appearance
3. Lack of direct references to "homosexuality"
4. Use of words to avoid the term "homosexuality"
5. Poor eye contact when discussing sensitive issues
Content:
1. Twenty-year-old college student
2. Self-reported isolation from women
3. Unhappy with homosexual feelings
4. Sees solution as "being made to change," that is, reliance on magical cure

Mrs. B.
Process:
1. Initially avoids discussion of issue of concern
2. Neat appearance, well dressed
3. Good eye contact, except when discussing sexual values
4. Rigid moral and value system

Content:
1. Forty-five-year-old housewife and mother of three teenage children
2. Unhappy over loss of control with children
3. Suspicious over not knowing details of daughter's dating experiences
4. Views herself as failure for not being the same type mother as her mother was
5. Sees solution as learning a better way to gain control over her children

Performance Exercises

1. Divide the group into triads with one interviewer, one client, and one observer. Use this format to practice confronting skills with a client who continues to ramble off on tangents. The observer should concentrate on specific verbal and nonverbal behaviors that are present whenever the interviewer attempts a confrontation.
2. Each individual should generate a specific preplanned format for a structured interview. Use the interview format in this chapter as a guideline. Role-play some short interviews in triads with an observer, interviewer, and client. The observer should concentrate on situations where the interviewer begins to counsel rather than interview and should provide feedback to the role-players. To develop added skill at structured interviewing, suggest that the role-playing client make every effort to get the interviewer to counsel rather than interview.
3. Practice role-playing the structured interview in triads to develop your note-taking abilities. When you have finished the interview, compare your notes with the observer for accuracy.

9

The Nonverbal Client

As we have previously discussed, open and honest communication is an essential ingredient in effective helping. Many clients experience considerable difficulty with this type of communication. These clients are often referred to by such labels as "resistant" or "passive." Because this kind of label can have pejorative connotations, we prefer to use the general term *nonverbal clients*.

In this chapter we will discuss the various types of nonverbal clients, describe possible positive and negative counselor reactions that nonverbal clients engender, and present effective questioning techniques by which to facilitate meaningful and productive communication. In no other area of helping is the skilled use of questioning more necessary to bring about the open and honest dialogue necessary to effective helping.

THE NONVERBAL CLIENT DEFINED

Practically all approaches to counseling (Combs, Avila, & Purkey, 1978; Dyer & Vriend, 1975; Krumboltz & Thoresen, 1969; Rogers, 1942) consider client volition—willingness to be an active participant in counseling—to be a necessary condition for effectiveness. Since the basic nature and process of counseling is essentially a verbal interchange between client and counselor, anything that exerts limitations on this verbal interchange will have impact on the counseling process.

Clients who are not especially verbal, fluent, or articulate pose certain difficulties for counselors attempting to facilitate the counseling process. These are the nonverbal clients.

When dealing with nonverbal clients, counselors must attempt to identify the possible reasons for this behavior and subsequently modify their verbal interaction techniques to accommodate the situation. Depending on the nature of the nonverbal behavior, this may entail confronting and encouraging the client to be more forthcoming in his or her discussions or it may require greater use of questions as a verbal interaction technique. Regardless of the reason, one fact will always be present: the counselor will have to assume an active role and make greater use of questions in counseling to facilitate the counseling process.

Vriend and Dyer (1973) offer a vivid description of the impact a nonverbal client can have on the counseling process:

> Many a practicum student has spent the night prior to his first interview asking for divine intervention in the granting of a cooperative, talkative client only to encounter the more common client, who is testy, overly restrained, feeling abused, or outright hostile. The fledgling counselor seldom forgets the sinking feelings of impotence that were engendered by his beginning struggles to be effective [p. 246].

TYPES OF NONVERBAL CLIENTS

Nonverbal clients can be identified functionally by two major categories: (1) Clients who simply do not possess the appropriate verbal skills necessary for "talking therapies." These include nontalkative clients, clients who are not verbally fluent, and young children. (2) Clients who are reluctant or resistant to the counseling process or who do not want to cooperate in the counseling venture.

Generally, both types of nonverbal clients will demonstrate a certain level of ambivalence at their inability to be cooperative, on the one hand wanting to solve their problems, and on the other, expressing reservations to cooperating with the tasks necessary to counseling.

Nontalkative Clients

The laconic, or verbally reserved, client will generally respond to talking therapies with short, terse, and succinct responses. Counselors sometimes react to this client by inferring some underlying resistance or lack of motivation for counseling, but not everyone who comes to counseling is verbally fluent or able to express him- or herself in verbal dialogue.

Many individuals are quiet and reserved in their verbal interactions. Their verbal behavior should not be taken as an indication of their level of cooperation or underlying resistance.

It should be remembered that clients who are not accustomed to talking about themselves at great lengths will hardly "open up" and become verbally fluent in the course of one or two interviews. To facilitate the process, the counselor will have to take the initiative and make inquiries into the significant issues relevant to the presenting problem.

The increased use of questions, most notably open-ended questions, is the easiest way to facilitate the verbal exchange with the nontalkative client. Using closed questions that require only a "yes" or "no" response should be avoided, since they will only further encourage brief responses. However, direct questions focused on eliciting specific information, and open-ended questions requiring the client to respond with whatever he or she feels important, can enhance progress in the counseling process. The following two counselor-client dialogues will demonstrate this point. The first dialogue is a counselor using the basic verbal interaction skills with a nonverbal client with little success; the second demonstrates the appropriate use of questions with the same client.

Dialogue A

Ms. Rich: So how did this make you feel?
Ramona: I don't know.
Mrs. Rich: I'll bet you were kind of upset.
Ramona: Yeah.
Ms. Rich: Does it still bother you to think about it?
Ramona: Not so much, now.
Mrs. Rich: I see. Well, what do you think you'd like to do about it the next time?
Ramona: Something different.
Ms. Rich: You'll want to change your reaction to it.
Ramona: I guess so.
Ms. Rich: Well, it must be difficult for you to think about that happening again.
Ramona: A little.

Dialogue B

Mr. Shelly: So how did it make you feel?
Stuart: I don't know.
Mr. Shelly: Well were you upset or irritated or just plain angry?
Stuart: I guess I was upset.
Mr. Shelly: Well, tell me what kinds of things you were thinking about. I mean, what was going through your mind at this time?

. . .

When you think back about it now, how do you feel?

. . .

Well, tell me a little more about how you and Jim got to know each other, for instance, how and where did you meet?

In the first dialogue, the counselor's attempts to reflect feelings or content were met with short, terse responses that had the tendency to close discussion of the issue, as is usually the case with nontalkative clients. This is really frustrating for counselors attempting to expand the level of discussion.

In the second dialogue, the counselor used little reflections, but employed the use of questions to enhance the verbal exchange. For many questions the counselor gave a verbal lead or suggestion to help start the client's response; for example, ". . . for instance, how and where did you meet?" This is an example of priming the client's verbal response and is sometimes necessary when using open-ended questions.

The effort is to get the client to start talking. The talking alone should help reinforce further verbal behavior. The crucial thing is to help the clients' verbal responses by reinforcing their efforts toward increased verbal fluency.

Young Children

Counselors working with elementary school children may find many nontalkative individuals among their clients. Getting the process underway with young children requires the ability to communicate at a level that is understandable to the child. Pietrofesa, Leonard, and Van Hoose (1978) suggest that some children come to counseling quite ready and eager to talk, while others sit or stand in silence. The second group requires flexibility and divergence from the standard, accepted verbal interaction responses of the counselor.

For the most part, children will verbalize their feelings (Hawkins, 1967; Van Hoose, 1966), provided the counselor can prime them with appropriate questions.

The Reluctant Client

Reluctant clients are those who would prefer not to be in counseling and not to talk about themselves (Eisenberg & Delaney, 1977). This includes the involuntary clients who are required to come to counseling, the family counseling clients who do not wish to be involved, the student who is referred for help, or the discipline problems in school settings. These clients can be hostile, contemptuous, extremely passive, silent, or as Redl (1966) adds, over-complaining.

With reluctant clients, there exists a genuine ambivalence about seeking help in the first place (Pietrofesa, Leonard, & Van Hoose, 1978):

> Counselee resistance to cooperation in the counseling endeavor may be a natural outgrowth of the client's ambivalence about growth and change.

Phenomenologically, the consistency of current behavior, while perhaps uncomfortable, offers security while behavior change, even though it may appear attractive, might make the client unsure . . . being pulled concurrently by behavior maintenance and behavior growth forces [p. 80].

Resorting to silence or short, terse comments is probably the most common type of reluctance and the type for which an increased level of questioning behaviors by the counselor will be the most useful verbal response. Open-ended and direct questions, as well as confronting and clarifying questions, can facilitate the nonverbal nature of this type of client.

NONVERBAL CLIENTS AND COUNSELING OUTCOMES

Clearly, nonverbal clients can exert a strong influence on the emotions of the counselor and ultimately upon the overall outcome of counseling. Several writers (Dyer & Vriend, 1975; Eisenberg & Delaney, 1977) have suggested that the presence of reluctant clients can engender counselor feelings of anxiety, incompetence, insecurity, and anger. When the counselor wishes to be successful and perceives that his or her efforts are being thwarted by an uncooperative client, anxiety may develop. Many counselors may be angry or irritated because the client is not behaving in the expected manner. In a sense, the counselor is perceiving the client as saying, "You're not good as a counselor and that's why I don't want to be here; therefore, I'm not going to cooperate" or "You can't help me" or even "I don't want to be here and I'm not going to play your silly game." Regardless of the client's actual intentions, silence or lack of cooperation can produce feelings of frustration in the counselor and thereby lessen the chances of a successful counseling outcome unless the reluctance is resolved.

Paradise (1978), in a study to determine the actual effects of client reluctance in counseling outcomes, found that clients high in precounseling reluctance reported significantly less satisfaction and improvement in their problem areas than clients who were low in reluctance. This finding is similar to other research demonstrating the counterproductive efforts of negative client expectations for counseling (Goodstein & Grigg, 1959; Wilkins, 1973).

Counselors fail to be effective with these clients. They fail to deal with the negative feelings and behaviors by avoiding or trying to change them. The most effective approach is to openly deal with the silent or uncooperative behaviors by using questions to openly confront the situation. An example will illustrate this point.

The Case of Mary

Mary is a 15-year-old high school student who has been ordered by a juvenile court to see a family counselor for her delinquent activities.

Counselor: How do you feel about coming here to see me every week?
Mary: I (pause) guess it's okay.
Counselor: Well, you don't seem to be enjoying this.
Mary: (silence)
Counselor: You can tell me how you're really feeling. It may help.
Mary: Okay, I guess I don't like this.
Counselor: Mary, why do you think the judge is making you see me?
Mary: (pause) I don't know. (pause) I don't care either. He's just hassling me.
Counselor: I can understand why you might feel the way you do, but we do have to spend this time together and I might be able to help a bit if you'd let me.
Mary: (silence)
Counselor: Why don't you tell me what you're thinking about now?
Mary: Nothing.
Counselor: Well, then, what would you like to be doing now? Is there something you'd like to see changed? You mentioned about being hassled—do you feel this is a hassle?
Mary: Yeah, I do.
Counselor: Well, how come people are hassling you?
Mary: (pause) I don't know—they just want to.
Counselor: Is there anything you're doing that makes them want to hassle you?
Mary: I guess—I don't know—I just don't want to be hassled by everyone.
Counselor: Well, why don't we use this time to work on ways to keep people from hassling you? Isn't that something you want to see changed?
Mary: Yeah, but I can't do anything about it.
Counselor: Well, that may not be true. Remember I asked you earlier why you thought the judge wanted you to see me. Do you think that what he wants is possibly similar to what you want?
Mary: Maybe, I don't know.
Counselor: Well, maybe we could talk about that. Could you tell me a little about the kinds of things that make you feel hassled?

In this excerpt, the counselor is actively directing questions toward the client in an effort to get her to start talking. The client's uncooperative behavior is obvious and, considering the involuntariness of the circumstances, is to be expected. Using open-ended questions and questions designed to confront the reluctant behavior of the client are excellent ways to begin to start dealing with the reluctance. Hopefully, if pursued, the client will begin to verbalize her negative feelings and the counselor can begin to work toward developing a relationship conducive to counseling progress. Using the traditional verbal techniques in this case, such as reflections and clarifications, would only allow the client's reluctant behaviors to continue.

As illustrated above, the counselor will have to assume much greater control and responsibility for the direction and focus of the interview. Without this increased counselor responsibility, at least until the reluctance is mediated, the entire process of counseling will fail to develop.

A more complete discussion of other techniques useful for working with reluctant clients can be found in Brammer and Shostrum (1968) and Eisenberg and Delaney (1977).

SUMMARY

Questions can be quite useful in counseling nonverbal clients. Generally, the use of open-ended, direct, and confronting questions can facilitate the verbal dialogue whenever the client is:

Nontalkative and silent
Reluctant and uncooperative

For the counseling process to develop appropriately, the counselor must facilitate the verbal dialogue by determining whether the reason for the nonverbal behavior is just a lack of verbal fluency or genuine reluctance that could prove detrimental to counseling effectiveness. If the latter is the case, then specific efforts must be undertaken to identify and resolve the sources of reluctance before any meaningful progress could be expected to occur.

EXERCISE 1

For each of the following case descriptions, identify whether the client is simply nontalkative or genuinely reluctant.

a. Frank is a 16-year-old who has not been successful in counseling. He was referred by his mother because she wanted him to start losing weight. While he feels badly about his obesity because his friends ridicule him, he enjoys being the biggest of his group. In counseling he does not seem to be cooperative in his verbal discussions related to his problem.

Is he reluctant or nontalkative and why? _____

_____

_____

b. Judith is a 13-year-old middle-school student who has been sent to
the guidance counselor for disruptive behavior in the classroom. She
has had numerous disciplinary actions against her for the past several years. Most of her trouble seems to stem from her inability to get
along with her classmates and follow the rules of the classroom. In
counseling she is hostile and unfriendly to the counselor stating, "I
don't have to talk to nobody, unless I want."

   Is she reluctant or nontalkative and why? _____

_____

_____

c. Louis is a 40-year-old chemical engineer who is having marital problems. He comes to the counselor at the request of his wife. She has
been seeing this counselor in family counseling for three weeks prior
to Louis's first session. While Louis wants to improve the marriage, he
finds it very difficult to discuss his personal problems with a stranger,
and thus the counselor is having a difficult time getting him to
verbalize some of his concerns.

   Is Louis reluctant or nontalkative and why? _____

_____

_____

EXERCISE 2

   For the following client statements, provide the best response.
After you have answered each of the responses, discuss your answers
and the reasons for each in small discussion groups.

a. Patty is a 14-year-old referred by the juvenile court for mandatory
counseling.
   "I don't have to come here. You can't help me. I don't have to
listen to your jive."

   Your response _____

_____

What types of feelings does her response engender? _____

_____

How would you describe her feelings? _____

_____

_____

b. George is a 30-year-old divorced father, who is trying to help his children, who have been in several minor scrapes with the juvenile authorities by seeing the family counselor.

"Look, I suppose you want me to tell you all about our divorce because you think that's why my kids are getting in trouble with the cops. Well, you can forget it; I'm here to discuss *them*, not *me*. So what do you want to know?"

Your response _____

_____

What types of feelings does his response engender? _____

_____

How would you describe his feelings? _____

_____

_____

c. Elise is an 18-year-old college sophomore who comes to the college counseling center for help in deciding what to major in at college.

"I don't want a career. I just want to pick a major. I don't know why you keep asking me all these questions; I just don't have answers for them."

Your response _____

_____

What types of feelings does her response engender? _____

_____

How would you describe her feelings? _____

_____

d. Norm is an 8-year-old who has been sent to the counselor for crying in class for no apparent reason.

"I don't know why I was sent here."

Your response _____

_____

What types of feelings does his response engender? _____

_____

How would you describe his feelings? _____

_____

_____

EXERCISE 3

For each of the following nonverbal clients, describe the underlying reasons for his or her nonverbal behavior, and suggest possible verbal techniques you could use to facilitate a counseling relationship with each. Discuss your answers in small groups.

a. A nontalkative elementary school child seeing a counselor for the first time in relation to several fights in the school yard

_____

_____

_____

b. A hostile parent of a young girl who refuses to discuss the girl's situation at home

_____

_____

_____

c. A shy teenage boy who is having problems making friends and finding dates with girls

_____

_____

_____

d. A formerly hospitalized, schizophrenic 40-year-old woman who is living in a half-way house and is withdrawn and suspicious whenever she talks about herself for fear that someone will send her back to the hospital

_____

_____

_____

e. An 18-year-old boy who is in a drug rehabilitation program because he'd rather be there than in jail

_____

_____

_____

10

Questions:
Overall Perspective

Questions constitute a large part of human interaction. They can be used to facilitate or inhibit communication. They communicate interest, express understanding, or share a concern. They can also threaten, confront, or demonstrate superiority. Because there is a learned risk in using them in the counseling relationship, questions have been neglected as a useful counseling skill.

We have shown, however, that questions are not without merit. Despite the inherent risk in their use, questions can greatly facilitate counseling interactions by inviting the client to speak, saving time, focusing the attention of the client, making general concepts more specific, or helping bind specific examples into general themes. Questions can help the client, making general concepts more specific, or helping bind specific examples into general themes. Questions can help the client process bits of information on higher conceptual levels. They can also assist the counselor in sorting out the hundreds of events that occur during the counseling session. Questions can even facilitate a warm trusting climate in which two partners strive to work toward mutually agreed-upon goals.

THE CONTEXT OF COUNSELING

We have defined counseling as a process of interaction undertaken to resolve specific agreed-upon problems. The questions discussed in this book have been used within that context. Counseling is based on the establishment and maintenance of a facilitated relationship; it demands the exchange of information that leads to new learning, unlearning, or relearning. This process then culminates and can be observed in constructive behavior change.

We have shown formal counseling as consistently progressing through regular and interdependent phases. The facilitative conditions of empathic understanding, respect, and genuineness continue throughout all phases of counseling. Occasionally action facilitatively precedes understanding. We have also outlined several phases in the counseling process; we did not intend to underscore discrete phases. Counseling is a developing process with a continuity of purpose to unify it.

Some people feel this approach to counseling is excessively logical. They argue that counseling is carried out in a relatively illogical, emotion-loaded fashion and that progression in a predetermined order curtails the client's ability to think or talk about relevant issues (Patterson, 1974). Yet we feel that counseling is more successful when it follows logical communication patterns. The client is more likely to remember all aspects of an issue and to cover it more thoroughly when it is approached systematically. Furthermore, the client is more likely to favorably adapt to responsibility in the relationship if there is some indication of the expectations of the counseling process (Hoehn-Saric et al., 1964; Long, 1968; Truax & Carkhuff, 1967). We believe the counselor should provide structure only to the extent necessary. If the client engages in appropriate behavior, there is no need for the client to be lectured on the counseling process. The counselor always influences his client's responses by replies (or lack of them). Whatever client statements the counselor responds to will be reinforced; conversely, whatever the counselor fails to respond to in the client tends to be extinguished. Because one of the functions of a counselor is to influence the content, manner, and sequencing of the client's communications, the counselor influence should follow a pattern.

Exploration

During the exploratory phase of the counseling process, the client and counselor exchange information about one another. This helps each establish the counselor-client relationship. We believe both client and counselor must find tentative replies to a series of questions, whether spoken or unspoken, about each other. During this phase, questions are frequently and appropriately used to invite client involvement in the process, to assist in establishing a genuine and comprehensible relationship, and to identify perceived areas of difficulty.

Integration

During the integrating phase of the counseling process, the client moves to a comprehensible understanding of self, world, and the difficulties in one's life. The client is prepared to directly move toward constructive behavior change. Questions are effectively used during this phase to help the client express underlying assumptions, give specific examples, outline the range of goals and the extent of available resources. Questions are also used to help the counselor understand the themes and patterns of the client's behavior, check out inferences about the client, and become acquainted with each client's particular attitudes, emotional/motivational forces, and concept of self. Questions can help clarify discrepancies perceived by the counselor and assist in determining whether the client is ready to accept the possibility of affecting real and positive change in behavior.

Action

During this phase, established goals are accomplished through constructive behavior change on the part of the client. Identifiable goals are outlined, resolving alternatives are listed and evaluated, a plan of action is selected, implemented, and evaluated before the client moves on and attempts the next alternative solution.

In our concept of counseling, insight is not enough. There must be changes in client behavior for counseling to be successful. While intrapersonal exploration is a basic client activity in counseling, changes in client behavior must accompany or follow development of self-awareness. Self-exploration leads both to self-awareness and to self-understanding of the intrapersonal processes. This understanding, in turn, frequently becomes the basis on which the client begins to act in more facilitative ways, so that behavior and understanding of self are congruent. This action is usually manifested first in the therapeutic setting, as the client experiments with new behaviors on the counselor.

Self-exploration reveals inconsistencies and contradictions for the client. The counselor uses questions to confront the client with attitudes, feelings, and behaviors that have been experienced but denied or distorted in awareness. As denied or distorted aspects of the self become symbolized in awareness, the client becomes more self-aware. Vague dissatisfactions become more specific. As the client becomes more aware of specific dissatisfactions as well as specific abilities, plans of action emerge to allow the client to bring behavior more in line with what the client wants. In other words, as the client develops a stronger understanding of self in an environment that does not elicit defensive behavior, it becomes increasingly important to bring behavior, attitudes, feelings, beliefs, and values in line to maintain internal congruence. The congruence provided by the counselor as a condition of therapy must become part of the client's change. Counselor questions help the client in self-exploration, which leads to the client's awareness of denied or distorted aspects of self. Questions help the client bring internal and external behavior into line with a more completely and clearly perceived and accepted self.

Questions indeed encourage the client toward self-expression and the cognitive processing of behavior, attitudes, feelings, beliefs, and values. Major critical client change follows from this understanding of self (Lieberman, Yalom, & Miles, 1973) and action on the part of the client (Carkhuff, 1969b). Understanding and action are interacting processes that often occur simultaneously (Carkhuff, 1969b). Either may precede or follow the other, depending on internal perceptions or external conditions. Nonspecific behavior changes can occur as byproducts of altered self-understanding and self-acceptance, or changes in self-understanding and acceptance can occur as byproducts of one's behavior change.

BASIC ASSUMPTIONS

Human beings can choose to change their behavior in conscious and deliberate ways as they understand themselves and their world. Human behavior also shapes them as existing organisms, altering the ways they must understand themselves in order to remain congruent.

The environment shapes human behaviors by providing both specific and limited choices or alternatives and by reinforcing certain responses while extinguishing others. So it is with the counseling relationship.

QUESTIONS

Questions fit in this context as part of the shaping process of counseling. They are a powerful and useful part of the mutual process of counseling. Whether the client or the counselor leads, together they progress toward increasingly understood and agreed-upon goals. The counselor, in other words, is not content with merely responding to what the client is trying to deal with; the counselor extends the client's leading edge in order to provide new dimensions toward which to stretch.

We agree with Patterson (1974) that continuous questioning by the counselor should be avoided. Stretching at anything will become exhausting, and continuous leading by the counselor will cause the client to fall into the position of respondee.

We also feel that there is a unique logic brought to the counseling relationship by each client in addition to the larger logic shared by people who exist within the same culture. The human logic is shared by all human beings. It is within the context of these logics that questions can be appropriately formulated.

QUESTIONS AND MODELING

We have outlined the range of questions from completely closed to those that progress through the process of recall, organization, and evaluation of experience to formulation of a reply. We have indicated that questions impose a range of limits including control of frame of reference, time frame, and background data supplied. We have suggested that questions can be useful invitations to the client to participate in the process and also are useful in directing the process.

We have offered cautions about the use of questions, while outlining their use in a variety of contexts—most notably, the structured interview. We have offered advice on the interpretations of replies to questions. We have indicated that questions must have a clear purpose and be related to the issue being discussed. And we have outlined the hallmarks of the facilitative question.

What we also want to do is point to questions as helping to model full human functioning. The counselor who replies only as responder, who avoids counseling leads, who labors through personal curiosity and multiple discrepancies while the client resolves questions is certainly modeling an example of limited human relating. The type of treatment we have espoused is one in which the counselor models behaviors for the client to perform. Such behaviors include leading as well as listening, disclosing as well as understanding, and resolving as well as tolerating. In this context, questioning not only is a useful tool, it becomes an essential element of all therapeutic interaction.

11

Group Activities

By now you should be reasonably competent in discriminating between facilitative and nonfacilitative questions. You should be able to recognize the different types of questions and understand their correct usage. But being able to select a helpful question is different from being able to formulate one yourself. This chapter will give you practice in listening to and formulating your own questions by incorporating the skills you have learned in this book.

In this section are small group activities. Each of the groups should be composed of professional helpers who have read this book. Members of the group are to "supervise" each other—that is, listen to and criticize the responses of the other members. Listen for the underlying communication in the questions being asked, and think about what is really being said. Discuss the follow-up questions and any other questions that arise. Use the group as a resource, and as a source of feedback about your own communication style.

The activities are arranged sequentially. The skills they seek to develop correspond to the three phases of counseling. You should complete all the activities in this chapter. If you skip some of them, try to maintain the order in which the activities are presented. The activities themselves are self-explanatory. All necessary materials are contained within the text.

ACTIVITY 1

Interviewing

Objectives.

1. To acquaint participants with the dynamics of questioning
2. To help participants understand one role of questions in obtaining information

Materials.

None

Time Required.

30 minutes

Procedure.

1. Break into dyads.
2. One member of the pair is to interview his or her partner. The purpose of the interview is to obtain as much information about the other person as possible. During the exchange the interviewer must exclusively ask questions. After five minutes the interview is stopped.
3. Participants switch roles. This interview is also stopped after five minutes.
4. Dyads will discuss the interview process. They should consider how much information was received and how the interviewee felt about the interview process.
5. Dyads will now interview each other again. This time the participants will try to obtain as much information about his or her partner without asking any questions at all. Each interview will again last a total of five minutes.
6. Partners will now discuss the interaction again.

Follow-Up.

1. How did you respond when you were being asked a long list of questions? How did you feel?
2. How did you respond when no questions were being presented to you? How did you feel?
3. Compare your reactions to the two situations. Which was more successful?
4. What types of questions did you ask?
5. Which were the most successful in obtaining information?

ACTIVITY 2

Beginning

Objectives.

1. To provide participants with a set of alternatives for beginning an interview
2. To help participants learn how to analyze the effectiveness of opening questions

Materials.

None

Time Required.

30 minutes

Procedure.

1. Break into groups of four to six participants.
2. Each group should appoint a recorder to take notes during the rest of the session.
3. The members of each group now brainstorm questions and statements that can be used to begin a counseling session. The questions or statements suggested should be appropriate opening statements after the client has entered and sat down in the counselor's office for the first time.
4. After all possible suggestions are recorded, the evaluation procedure begins. Members of the group should discuss each of the suggested alternatives for interest and respect communicated to the client. The amount of freedom of response communicated to the client should also be discussed.
5. After each of the suggested opening statements are evaluated this way, the group should "star" the two best alternatives, who communicate the most interest in and respect for the client, as well as provide the client with a great deal of freedom of response.
6. Each group of participants should write its two best opening statements on the blackboard.

Follow-Up.

1. Is there any similarity to the opening statements selected?
2. Are there any other characteristics that they all seem to have?

3. Are there any other qualities that you think are critical to a good opening counselor statement?
4. How important do you think the counselor's initial statement is to the entire counseling process?

ACTIVITY 3

Formulating Questions

Objectives.

1. To give students practice in formulating different types of questions
2. To help students analyze different types of questions
3. To demonstrate the relationship between them

Materials.

Stimulus Statements for formulating questions

Time Required.

40 minutes

Procedure.

1. Break into groups of four to six participants.
2. Provide each group with a copy of the stimulus statements.
3. One member of the group reads Stimulus Statement A to the rest of the group.
4. Group members brainstorm a series of questions they would ask Client A in response to the stimulus statement as if they were the counselor. A recorder, appointed by the group, records all suggestions.
5. Each question suggested is evaluated in terms of the amount of empathic understanding and respect it communicates. Suggestions should be made on how to increase the empathic understanding and respect communicated by the questions.
6. The procedure is repeated for Stimulus Statement B.

Follow-Up.

1. How effective are questions in communicating empathy and respect?
2. What types of questions have a higher empathic communication than others?
3. How effective were you in communicating empathy and respect in the form of questions?

STIMULUS STATEMENTS FOR FORMULATING QUESTIONS

Stimulus Statement A

I guess I really don't have any energy. You know, I can't seem to do anything. All I want to do is sleep. My husband is really getting mad at me, but I don't even care. I've never felt this way before.

Stimulus Statement B

I don't understand why she got so angry with me. I only had a couple of drinks. I always have a few drinks before I go home. I mean, you'd think I was out with another woman or something. She's really starting to get on my nerves.

ACTIVITY 4

Integrating Questions

Objective.

1. To give students practice in incorporating questions into their counseling style

Materials.

Pencil, paper

Time Required.

One hour

Procedure.

1. Break into triads.
2. Each triad will appoint one member to be a counselor, one member a client, and one member an observer.
3. The client will use an original problem during the counseling interaction.
4. The counselor and client will proceed as though this is the initial counseling session.
5. The observer will record all questions asked by the counselor during this interview. The observer should stop the interaction after about ten minutes.
6. The observer should read each question the counselor asked to the other two members of the group. The triad will then discuss each question. Attention should be paid to the type of question, its function, and its effect on the client.
7. Members switch roles and repeat the process two more times.

Follow-Up.

1. How many questions did the average counselor ask during the ten-minute session?
2. What types of questions were asked?
3. What was the most common type of question?
4. Were most of the questions open or closed?
5. What effect did questions seem to have on the client?

ACTIVITY 5

Formulating Open Questions

Objectives.

1. To provide participants with practice in formulating open questions
2. To provide participants with practice in changing closed questions to open questions

Materials.

Stimulus statements with closed questions

Time Required.

30 minutes

Procedure.

1. Break into groups of four to six.
2. Give each participant a copy of the stimulus statements with closed questions.
3. Each group will discuss the closed questions provided and reformulate them into open questions.
4. After the format of all the closed questions has been changed, participants will read the questions and evaluate their significance to the client.
5. Additional significant open questions can be added to the list.

Follow-Up.

1. How difficult was it to reformulate closed questions into open questions?
2. How did reformulating the questions increase their significance to the client?
3. How can you remind yourself to evaluate the significance of a question before asking it?

STIMULUS STATEMENTS WITH CLOSED QUESTIONS

Stimulus Statement A

"I don't know what to do. I'm afraid of people. Afraid of getting too close to them. I mean I like people, I just don't know what to do. I think I like them too much. I start to get to know someone and it's okay. Then I fall head over heals for them. It scares me. I always wind up getting hurt. That's how it happened before. That's how it happened with Jim."

Closed Questions.

1. How many times did this happen before?
2. Would you say you were in love with Jim?
3. You'd like me to tell you what to do?
4. Are you afraid of people hurting you or you hurting people?
5. Was Jim in love with you?

Stimulus Statement B

"I don't know what to do. My husband's going to be out in the desert all summer mining. He wants me to go out there and spend the summer with him. I'm kind of scared. I've never been in the desert. Plus if I stay here I can work at summer camp and earn some money which we desperately need. But then I might not see him for months!"

Closed Questions.

1. Where is your husband mining?
2. How long will he be gone?
3. What are you afraid of?
4. How much money do you make at summer camp?
5. How much money is your husband earning mining?

ACTIVITY 6

Two-Start Exercise

Objective.

1. To compare the impact of a counseling session on each participant if the counselor uses fact or opinion questions (selected from the closed end of the questioning spectrum) or broad descriptive questions (selected from the open end of the questioning spectrum)

Materials.

None

Time Required.

25–30 minutes

Procedure.

1. Each person selects a partner.
2. Partners decide who will initially be client and who counselor.
3. The client selects a vivid experience in his or her life that had a definite impact.
4. The counselor begins the session with a fact or opinion question selected from the more closed end of the questioning spectrum; for example, "When did this experience occur?"
5. The counselor continues attempting to facilitate the interview using fact or opinion questions.
6. After the session has progressed for several minutes (three to five), stop the interview.
7. The counselor then begins the interview again, but this time uses broad descriptive questions from the more open end of the questioning spectrum; for example, "Will you tell me about your experience in your own words?"
8. Stop the role-play after a few client-counselor interactions (three to five minutes).
9. Have the partners change roles and repeat steps 3 through 8.
10. Compare client-counselor reactions to the two different beginnings.
11. The whole process may be repeated several times with new partners.

Follow-Up.

1. How did the client feel when the counselor tried to lead the session

with closed facts or opinion questions? With open, descriptive questions?

2. How did the counselor feel in playing out each questioning role?
3. Which type of questions appeared to generate the most useful information?
4. Which type of questions appeared to foster a closer personal relationship between client and counselor?
5. Which type of questions were easier for the counselor to formulate?
6. Are you beginning to recognize the impact of different types of questions and to be flexible in using both types?

ACTIVITY 7

Interview Outline Exercise

Objective.

1. To teach the counselor the advantages and disadvantages of having a planned outline of important information needed before entering a session

Materials.

None

Time.

25–30 minutes

Procedure.

1. Each person selects a partner.
2. Partners decide who will initially play client and who counselor.
3. The client and counselor select together a general topic that appears to have meaning for both of them.
4. The counselor begins the session on the topic selected without having a planned outline. Begin with a broad or open-ended question.
5. Base all further questions or statements on the client's responses. See how long you can go without introducing a new topic.
6. Stop after about five minutes and critique the counselor's performance.
7. Role-play a counseling session on a topic that appears to have meaning for both client and counselor, but this time before starting the role-play the counselor should make up an outline of three or four specific questions which he or she thinks are logically related to the topic at hand.
8. Do the second interview trying to keep a balance between insightful probing and accomplishing your preplanned outline.
9. Stop after about five minutes and critique the counselor's performance.
10. Let the partners reverse roles and repeat steps 3 through 9.
11. Compare client-counselor reactions to the two different strategies.

Follow-Up.

1. Which interview appeared to progress more logically? Which gave evidence of greater counselor control?

2. Using which strategy did the counselor appear to feel more comfortable?
3. What logical and/or emotional factors were you aware of during each of the role-plays?
4. Do you think it is better to develop some questions that you have at hand at the outset of each session, whether or not you use them?
5. Under which condition did the interview appear to progress furthest, with least resistence?

ACTIVITY 8

Goal Setting

Objectives.

1. To help participants understand the process of setting goals that are meaningful, realistic, and attainable
2. To give participants the opportunity to formulate goals using questions

Materials.

None

Time Required.

15–20 minutes

Procedure.

1. Participants should be divided into small groups of four or five.
2. Each individual should formulate a short-term goal to work toward.
3. The small groups should be further divided into dyads, with one individual as the counselor and the other as the client.
4. The counselor should use questions to help the client evaluate goals in terms of being meaningful, realistic, and attainable.

Follow-Up.

1. What types of questions were used most in the discussion of goals?
2. How did the counselor help determine if the goal was meaningful, realistic, and attainable?
3. How did the use of questions help to keep you focused on the task of goal-setting?
4. Could any other verbal techniques be used to accomplish the same objectives?

ACTIVITY 9

Generating Courses of Action

Objective.

1. To help the participants learn to generate possible courses of action related to a particular client problem

Materials.

Stimulus problems for generating courses of action

Time Required.

15–20 minutes

Procedure.

1. Participants should be divided into small groups of three or four.
2. For each of the stimulus problems, generate as many viable options as possible and discuss them with the total group.
3. During the group discussion, participants should be cognizant of the number and types of questions that are used to determine the viability of a given option.

Follow Up.

1. What types of questions were used to generate additional options and check the viability of participants' stated options?
2. How did the questions stimulate further options?

STIMULUS PROBLEMS FOR GENERATING COURSES OF ACTION

1. Margaret is a 23-year-old graduate student who is under some pressure from her boyfriend to move in with him. While she feels that those living arrangements would be fine, she is also afraid that her parents would not approve. She has to resolve the situation in some way.
2. Joshua is a 20-year-old college junior who is undecided about a major. While he enjoys English literature courses, he realizes that the job market in that area is not too promising. His parents are urging him to go into business administration because of the better job outlook, but he doesn't have much interest in business courses.
3. Rob is considering going back to school to finish his bachelor's degree. He has two more years of course work to complete. However, he doesn't have sufficient funds to go full-time and he doesn't think that going part-time would be a wise choice.
4. Nancy is a 14-year-old high school junior who has a friend who is selling drugs to school children. She has been debating whether she should turn this person in to the authorities. She has tried to talk to the person, urging him to stop, but has met with failure. She is afraid her own sister will start using drugs if something isn't done.

ACTIVITY 10

Evaluating Options

Objective.

1. To facilitate an understanding of the elements in evaluating options.

Materials.

Stimulus categories (below)

Time Required.

20–25 minutes

Procedure.

1. Divide the participants into small groups of four or five.
2. Instruct each individual to construct a hypothetical problem situation together with potential options to resolve the problem.
3. Each participant should present a problem together with the options, and discuss the evaluation of the options in terms of the stimulus categories presented below. Particular attention should be paid to the use of questions to inquire about these categories.

Stimulus Categories.

1. Needs
2. Consequences, both positive and negative
3. Attitudes and beliefs
4. Value systems
5. Probability and possibility of consequences
6. Alternative actions as a result of consequences

Follow-Up.

1. What types of questions were used to evaluate the options?
2. Did questioning contribute to greater understanding of these options?
3. Did the questions stimulate the closer evaluation of the options?

A Final Note

Using questions appropriately is a difficult task even for the experienced helper. The decision to use questions is never without its liabilities. Questions always carry the risk of threatening the client and increasing his or her defensiveness. If not used carefully, they shift the responsibility of counseling from the client to the counselor. Questions can also limit client spontaneity by restricting his or her communication to responses to specific counselor questions. Asking questions also risks directing the counselor-client communication to less critical areas, since the counselor is hypothesizing what is important to the client.

However, in spite of all these liabilities, questions are critical tools throughout the counseling process. They can be used effectively during a structured interview or screening situation to obtain specific information about the client, as well as to make judgments about counselor response styles. They are also useful during the counseling stages of exploration, integration, and action. They help the client disclose more freely, have a better understanding of self, and behave more appropriately.

The dangers and limits of questioning can best be overcome through understanding the counseling process. Questions are evaluated in terms of the long- and short-term goals of counseling and how well they facilitate or impede those goals.

Counselors should carefully study the reactions of each client to each question. Serious counselors will find it useful to tape counseling sessions and to evaluate questioning skills. By classifying the questions asked, counselors will gain insight into what types of question they most frequently ask. Counselors should also rate the client's level of disclosure to the different types of questions. Any defensiveness on the part of the client should especially be noted. Questions can be helpful but, like any other counseling tool, they should continually be evaluated for effectiveness.

References

Anderson, R., & Biddle, W. On asking people questions about what they are reading. In G. H. Bowes (Ed.), *The psychology of learning and motivation: Advances in research and theory*. New York: Academic Press, 1975.

Anthony, W. A. The relationship between human relationship skills and an index of psychological adjustment. *Journal of Counseling Psychology*, 1973, *20*, 489–490.

Benjamin, A. *The helping interview*. Boston: Houghton Mifflin, 1969.

Berenson, B., & Carkhuff, R. R. *Sources of gain in counseling and psychotherapy*. New York: Holt, Rinehart & Winston, 1967.

Berne, E. *Games people play*. New York: Grove Press, 1964.

Blocher, D. *Developmental counseling*. New York: Ronald Press, 1966.

Brammer, L. M. *The helping relationship: Process and skills*. Englewood Cliffs, N.J.: Prentice-Hall, 1973.

Brammer, L. M. *The helping relationship*. (2nd ed.). Englewood Cliffs, N.J.: Prentice-Hall, 1979.

Brammer, L. M., & Shostrum, E. *Therapeutic psychology* (2nd ed.). Englewood Cliffs, N.J.: Prentice-Hall, 1968.

Carkhuff, R. R. *Helping and human relations: A primer for lay and professional helpers. Vol. I: Selection and training*. New York: Holt, Rinehart & Winston, 1969. (a)

Carkhuff, R. R. *Helping and human relations: A primer for lay and professional helpers. Vol. II: Practice and research*. New York: Holt, Rinehart & Winston, 1969. (b)

Carkhuff, R. R. *The art of helping*. Amherst, Mass.: Human Resource Development Press, 1972. (a)

Carkhuff, R. R. The development of a systematic human resource development model. *Counseling Psychologist*, 1972, *3*, 4–30. (b)

Carkhuff, R. R. *The art of problem-solving*. Amherst, Mass.: Human Resource Development Press, 1973.

Carkhuff, R. R., & Berenson, B. *Beyond counseling and therapy* (2nd ed.). New York: Holt, Rinehart & Winston, 1977.

Combs, A., Avila, D., & Purkey, W. *Helping relationships* (2nd ed.). Boston: Houghton Mifflin, 1978.

Corey, G. *Theory and practice of counseling and psychotherapy*. Monterey, Calif.: Brooks/Cole, 1977.

Crary, W. G., & Johnson, C. W. The mental status examination. In C. W. Johnson, J. R. Snibbe, & L. E. Evans (Eds.), *Basic psychotherapy: A programmed text.* New York: Spectrum, 1975.

Delaney, D. J., & Eisenberg, S. *The counseling process.* Chicago: Rand McNally, 1972.

Dyer, W., & Vriend, J. *Counseling techniques that work.* Washington, D.C.: APGA Press, 1975.

Eaton, M. T. & Peterson, M. *Psychiatry* (2nd ed.). Flushing, N.Y.: Medical Examination Press, 1969.

Egan, G. *The skilled helper.* Monterey, Calif.: Brooks/Cole, 1975.

Eisenberg, S., & Delaney, D. *The counseling process* (2nd ed.). Chicago: Rand McNally, 1977.

Enelow, A., & Wexler, M. *Psychiatry in the practice of medicine.* New York: Oxford Press, 1966.

Estes, S. G. Judging personality from expressive behavior. *Journal of Abnormal Social Psychology,* 1938, *33,* 217–236.

Eysenck, H. J. The effects of psychotherapy: An evaluation. *Journal of Consulting Psychology,* 1952, *16,* 319–324.

Eysenck, H. J. The effects of psychotherapy. In H. J. Eysenck (Ed.), *Handbook of abnormal psychology.* New York: Basic Books, 1960.

Eysenck, H. J. The effects of psychotherapy. *International Journal of Psychiatry,* 1965, *1,* 97–178.

Gazda, G., Asbury, F., Balzer, F., Childers, W., & Walters, R. *Human relations development* (2nd ed.). Boston: Allyn & Bacon, 1977.

Goodstein, L. D., & Grigg, A. E. Client satisfaction, counselors, and the counseling process. *Personnel and Guidance Journal,* 1959, *38,* 19–24.

Gordon, T. *Teacher effectiveness training.* New York: David McKay Co., 1974.

Hawkins, S. The content of elementary counseling interviews. *Elementary School Guidance and Counseling,* 1967, *2,* 114–120.

Hoehn-Saric, H., Frank, J. W., Imber, S. D., Nash, E. H., Stone, A. R., & Battle, C. L. Systematic preparation of patients for psychotherapy. *Journal of Psychiatry Research,* 1964, *2,* 267–281.

Ivey, A. *Micro-counseling.* Springfield, Ill.: Charles C Thomas, 1971.

Kahn, R., & Cannell, C. *The dynamics of interviewing (Theory, technique and cases).* New York: Wiley, 1957.

Kelly, E. L., & Fiske, D. W. *The prediction of performance in clinical psychology.* Ann Arbor: University of Michigan Press, 1951.

Krumboltz, J. D., & Thoresen, C. F. *Behavioral counseling: Cases and techniques.* New York: Holt, Rinehart & Winston, 1969.

Levy, B. I., & Ulman, E. Judging psychopathology from paintings. *Journal of Psychology,* 1967, *72*(2), 182–187.

Lieberman, M. A., Yalom, I. D., & Miles, M. B. *Encounter groups: First facts.* New York: Basic Books, 1973.

Long, L. *The effects of preteaching teacher interaction style on student achievement.* Unpublished doctoral dissertation, University of Illinois, Champaign-Urbana, 1975.

Long, T. J. *The effects of preteaching procedures on client behavior during initial counseling interviews.* Unpublished doctoral dissertation, Arizona State University, Tempe, 1968.

Long, T. J. A philosophical superstructure for an approach to counseling. In D. Delaney and T. Long (Eds.), *Readings in counseling and psychotherapy*. New York: Selected Academic Readings, 1969.

Luft, J. Implicit hypotheses and clinical predictions. *Journal of Social psychology*, 1959, *45*, 756–759.

Maloney, M., & Ward, M. *Psychological assessment*. New York: Oxford Press, 1976.

Marshall, D. *Adjunct questioning as a vehicle for improving memory during psychological counseling*. Unpublished doctoral dissertation, University of Illinois, Champaign-Urbana, 1976.

Maslow, A. *Toward a psychology of being* (2nd ed.). New York: D. Van Nostrand, 1968.

Middlebrooks, B. A principal humanizes his school. *Peabody Journal of Education*, 1975, *53*(1), 24–26.

Okun, B. F. *Effective helping: Interviewing and counseling techniques*. North Scituate, Mass.: Duxbury Press, 1976.

Paradise, L. V. *Client reluctance and counseling effectiveness*. Paper presented to the annual meeting of the American Education Research Association. Toronto, April 1978.

Patterson, C. H. *Humanistic education*. Englewood Cliffs, N.J.: Prentice-Hall, 1973. (a)

Patterson, C. H. *Theories of counseling and psychotherapy* (2nd ed.). New York: Harper & Row, 1973. (b)

Patterson, C. H. *Relationship counseling and psychotherapy*. New York: Harper & Row, 1974.

Pierce, R., & Drasgow, J. Teaching facilitative interpersonal functioning to psychiatric inpatients. *Journal of Counseling Psychology*, 1969, *16*(4), 295–298.

Pietrofesa, J., Leonard, G., & Van Hoose, W. H. *The authentic counselor* (2nd ed.). Chicago: Rand McNally, 1978.

Redl, F. *When we deal with children*. New York: Free Press, 1966.

Rogers, C. R. *Counseling and psychotherapy*. Boston: Houghton Mifflin, 1942.

Rogers, C. R. *Client-centered therapy*. Boston: Houghton Mifflin, 1951.

Rogers, C. R. The necessary and sufficient conditions of therapeutic personality change. *Journal of Consulting Psychology*, 1957, *21*, 95–103.

Rogers, C. R. *On becoming a person*. Boston: Houghton Mifflin, 1961.

Rogers, C. R. Empathic: An unappreciated way of being. *The Counseling Psychologist*, 1975, *5*(2), 2–10.

Shertzer, B., & Stone, S. C. *Fundamentals of counseling* (3rd ed.). Boston: Houghton Mifflin, 1980.

Soskin, W. F. Bias in postdiction and projective tests. *Journal of Abnormal Social Psychology*, 1954, *49*, 69–74.

Taft, R. The ability to judge people. *Psychological Bulletin*, 1955, *52*, 1–23.

Truax, C. B. *Counseling and psychotherapy: Process and outcome*. V.R.A. Research and Demonstration Grant #906-D, June 1966.

Truax, C. B., & Carkhuff, R. R. *Toward effective counseling and psychotherapy: Training and practice*. Chicago: Aldine, 1967.

Truax, C. B., & Mitchell, K. M. Research in certain therapist skills in relation to process and outcome. In A. E. Bergin & S. L. Garfield (Eds.), *Handbook of psychotherapy and behavior change: An empirical analysis.* New York: Wiley, 1971.

Van Hoose, W. H. Counseling with children. American Educational Research Association Abstracts. Washington, D.C.: American Educational Research Association, 1966.

Vriend, J., & Dyer, W. Counseling the reluctant client. *Journal of Counseling Psychology,* 1973, *20*(3), 240–246.

Wedell, C., & Smith, K. V. Consistency of interview methods in appraisal of attitudes. *Journal of Applied Psychology,* 1951, *35,* 392–396.

Weiss, J. H. Effect of professional training and amount and accuracy of information on behavioral predictions. *Journal of Consulting Psychology,* 1963, *27,* 257–262.

Wilkins, W. Expectancy and therapeutic gain. *Journal of Consulting and Clinical Psychology,* 1973, *40*(1), 69–77.

Index

3608

DATE DUE